The Simple Path to Anxious Attachment Recovery

Overcome the Fear of Abandonment, Develop Unshakeable Self-Confidence, and Nurture Fulfilling & Secure Relationships

Amara & Samir Everbond

Contents

Personal Note from Amara Everbond

∞

I know all too well the haunting echoes of a relentless fear of abandonment, the insatiable need for reassurance, and the overpowering belief that my self-worth hinged on the fickle nature of my relationship. My husband was once my entire world. I placed him on a pedestal, overlooking his flaws, and thoughts echoed in my mind, declaring, "I can't live without him" or "I would be nothing without him."

Unbeknownst to me, these toxic thoughts were robbing me of joy, symptomatic of a fear of abandonment and a deep desire to be loved. My understanding shifted when I delved into attachment styles, realizing I possessed the innate qualities of an anxious attachment style. This awareness liberated me from the habitual patterns I learned in childhood, and it was time to have my mindset grow up.

I discovered that I didn't have to cling to my husband as I did with my parents—a realization pivotal for our relationship and my personal growth. I once perceived independence as underrated, avoiding it and convincing myself that my anxious thoughts were pursuing unity and harmony with my husband. I thought my anxious attachment way of being was actually a spiritual journey of becoming one with him.

My transformation took a significant turn with the insights from Byron Katie's Four Questions[1] and a deeper understanding of the ego. I realized I am not my thoughts; they are subconscious habits, not conscious choices. I am the observer, not the thoughts themselves. I choose my actions, words, and ways of being. It's only when I attach myself to the anxious thought, allowing it to define me and dictate my actions, that I become trapped in its grip.

Then it all clicked for me: attachment styles are not identities but products of our ego-trained thoughts. We are the observers with the power to question these thoughts and remind ourselves of the truth. By questioning our attachment styles and challenging the thoughts that fuel them, we can break free from the limitations they impose on us. This realization empowered me to cultivate healthier ways of relating to others and myself based on conscious choices rather than subconscious habits. It opened up a world of possibilities for personal growth and transformation.

With this newfound understanding of myself, I started to support others who knew me before and after the shift. With a waitlist of potential clients, I followed the call and became a relationship coach.

After becoming a relationship coach, Samir and I traveled the world, gaining clients from diverse backgrounds. Guiding those with anxious attachment tendencies through the steps that led to my secure attachment awakening—the same steps we share in this book. The names and identities of the case studies in this book have been changed to preserve the privacy of those clients.

Samir witnessed my journey and observed the transformative impact on our clients' relationships, contributing to the writing of this book. It's designed to help anxious attachers and their partners approach their loved ones with empathy.

Remember, this is a journey. While I wish this book could eradicate anxious thoughts, only you can apply the knowledge, question your thoughts, and become a secure attacher.

I wish you resilience, self-discovery, and the profound joy that comes with securing your emotional well-being.

With Love,

Amara Everbond

Introduction

In our fast-paced and interconnected world of modern relationships, one simple text message can make or break a relationship in as little time as it takes to hit the 'send' button. Marika, a bright and ambitious young professional, knows this all too well. On a seemingly ordinary Tuesday evening, Marika sends her partner, Alan, a heartfelt text expressing her love and appreciation. A feeling of worry sweeps over her as she clicks the 'send' button. She glances at her phone, waiting for a response.

Minutes turn into what feels like hours, and with each passing second, her heart pounds louder in her chest. Negative thoughts flood her mind, making her question whether she said something wrong or if Alan has grown tired of her.

As the clock continues to tick the evening away, Marika's anxiety peaks. She can't focus on anything else, constantly checking her phone, hoping for a reply to calm her racing mind. She feels increasingly distant from Alan, convinced that her text triggered his withdrawal.

Finally, late into the night, her phone chimed. Alan responded, “Sorry I took so long to answer. I have been attending meeting after meeting today. I will call you when I get home. Love you, too!”

A flood of relief washes over Marika, but simultaneously, she can’t shake the lingering anxiety that consumed her entire evening. She struggles to find an answer that will match the calm coming through Alan’s text message, but ultimately, she drops the phone, feeling the weight of the last few hours pushing down on her chest.

This situation isn’t an isolated incident in Marika’s life or even isolated from her relationship with Alan. It is a recurring pattern that showcases her tussles with anxious attachment. She desperately seeks validation and security in her relationship, but her anxious thoughts, fueled by fears of rejection and abandonment, often lead her to overthink and misunderstand.

Can you relate to Marika’s plight? If so, you are not alone. Approximately 20% of the population experiences anxious attachment[2]. Yep, that’s right—one in five of us is rocking that vibe, and it can sneak into our romantic lives and how we interact with our partners.

Like Marika, you might be waiting for a reply to your text message. Oh boy, the struggle is real! Seconds turn into minutes, minutes into hours, and suddenly, you’re questioning life’s biggest mysteries:

"Did my message get lost in cyberspace?"

"Am I even worth a response?"

"Is my partner secretly plotting a disappearance?"

But texting isn't the only battlefield for anxiety. The feelings can rear their ugly heads in seemingly innocent ways, like when your romantic partner mentions having plans with friends over the weekend. This harmless remark can trigger a wild ride of emotions for someone with an anxious attachment. Cue the internal monologue:

"Does this mean he doesn't want to spend time with me?"

"Am I not fun enough?"

"Maybe she's secretly trying to get away from me!"

This turmoil doesn't remain confined to your mental landscape or your emotions. It affects you physically, too. Your heart starts racing, and your palms sweat as you desperately seek reassurance, like a detective searching for clues.

"You still want to hang out with me, right?" you casually throw in, trying to play it cool while secretly hoping they'll assure you they'd rather spend eternity with you than hang out with anyone else.

Sometimes, this person doesn't understand you need that reassurance—heck, sometimes, we're in the dark about our needs, too—and it might not come.

There are also moments of overthinking. You receive a sweet love note from your partner, expressing their affection and admiration for you. Instead of basking in the warmth of love, your brain analyzes every word and punctuation mark, searching for hidden meanings. "He didn't put an exclamation mark at the end. Does that mean he's not as excited about me as before? Did I do something wrong?!"

Oh, the drama! The good news is that you're not alone in this comedy of attachment errors. Countless individuals find themselves dancing this awkward but endearing tango with anxious attachment. The key is recognizing these patterns in everyday interactions and laughing at ourselves a little!

Only then can you move on to healthier, happier pastures; we are here to help you take those next steps. Like you, we are on a journey, and ours involves assisting individuals like you to tackle and overcome the struggles of anxious attachment. Do you know what fuels our fire? Seeing you and others break free from fear and insecurity and build unshakable self-confidence. We are all about nurturing the fulfilling and secure relationships we all deserve.

This book is not just a passive read; it's a dynamic exploration of yourself and your relationships. Within these pages, you'll find actionable steps, thought-provoking journal prompts, and valuable key takeaways at the end of each critical section.

Imagine each section as a "day" of personal growth dedicated to understanding and nurturing your attachment style. Whether you read this book in one sitting or savor each section at your own pace, you're in control.

Our goal is to guide you from an anxious attachment style toward a secure one. This transformation is not an overnight process. Instead, it's a progression of growth. Each step brings you closer to the security and emotional freedom you deserve in your relationships.

So, as you dive into each chapter, remember that this is your path to change. Embrace the practical steps, engage with the journal prompts, and absorb the key takeaways. Your commitment to this process will be your compass, leading you to a more secure attachment style and a happier, healthier you.

We have poured our heart and soul into crafting this simple, step-by-step, and practical guide with the ultimate aim of helping you overcome the anxious attachment tendencies we all deal with from time to time. The thorough approach to crafting the words in these pages is tailored just for you, regardless of whether you're a woman or a man (or any other gender). This isn't some cookie-cutter advice—no, we're all unique, and this guide respects and embraces that, something highlighted by the inclusive and culturally diverse real-life examples featured in the coming pages.

Let us give you a heads-up before we go any further. Sometimes, while reading this book, emotions may arise. It could be anxiety or guilt. There may be a rush of thoughts pushing at the walls of your mind simultaneously as you relate to the real-life examples illustrated. Don't fret. It's okay. Emotions are not bad things. They exist to guide you because they indicate that there is something within you that needs to be addressed. That is why you are here, after all. So, keep reading, and we will guide you to understanding what these emotions are trying to tell you.

Not just that. We've got you covered with more amazing answers! Get ready to learn coping tools like a pro to help you conquer anxiety. We'll dive deep into strategies for establishing trust in yourself and your relationships because trust is the backbone of healthy connections.

Oh, and setting healthy boundaries? Get set to master that like a boss! No more feeling overwhelmed or losing yourself in relationships. You'll have the tools to identify and manage those tricky triggers that keep messing with your inner peace. We're working on building that self-esteem of yours until it's soaring!

This guide is for you and everyone else who's grappling with anxious attachment issues. We're all in this together! But hey, if you're a therapist or a mental health professional seeking some excellent resources, this book's got you covered, too. And for those just into personal growth and healing, welcome aboard—there's something special here for you as well!

Laughter is the best medicine, and we have deliberately taken a lighthearted approach to broaching this tricky subject matter with you. We've all shed enough tears because of pain and sorrow, but the future remains bright as long as we can smile. Let us interject with our most serious voice to say this: We want you to know that you are not alone in this journey. We understand those struggles all too well and are here with you every step of the way. In this book, We have created a safe space where you can feel understood and embraced because we are your cheerleader, confidant, and unwavering support.

It can be daunting to face anxious attachment tendencies head-on, but trust us when we say you can conquer them. This journey will have ups and downs, but commit to it wholeheartedly. You deserve the freedom from anxiety, the joy of secure connections, and the unshakeable self-confidence that awaits you.

We won't sugarcoat it—overcoming anxious attachment requires consistent effort, but change is possible once you implement the strategies outlined in this book. Take those tiny steps every day; before you know it, you'll look back and see your incredible progress.

Every little step matters and every small victory deserves celebration. Be gentle with yourself as we explore and heal together. When setbacks occur, acknowledge them, learn from them, and return to becoming the best version of yourself possible.

As we close this introduction, I want you to hold on to a sense of hope and optimism. Change is not just a distant dream—it's a real possibility for you. You have the courage within to face these challenges. With each page you turn, with each insight you gain, you'll discover strength and resilience within you that you might not have known you had.

So, please take a deep breath, beautiful soul, and let's embark on this journey together. Let's embrace the possibilities of growth and healing and write a story of triumph and empowerment. We believe in you and your progress in becoming the incredible person you will bloom into as you unravel the layers of anxious attachment. You've got this!

Now, with smiles, let's jump right into Chapter 1.

Peeling Back the Layers

The Psychology of Anxious Attachment

∞

Imagine moving through a crowded street fair with music, laughter, and vibrant colors. You're holding hands with your partner, feeling content and secure. But suddenly, a wave of anxiety crashes over you like a tidal wave. Did he just glance at a woman who walked by? This woman is attractive, you think. More than you? The thoughts spiral and lead to doubt that this person loves you. You feel this moment is a charade, and they will leave you. These intrusive thoughts overwhelm you, and the joyful atmosphere around you feels suffocating—this torment is what many with anxious attachments endure.

Anxious attachment is more than just wanting to be close to someone or fearing a temporary period of singleness. It goes much deeper—an ingrained fear of abandonment, a haunting belief that those we love will inevitably leave us. This fear stems from our early experiences with caregivers, like the roots of a tree shaping how it grows.

Anxious attachment presents itself differently in everyone who relates to it, but common signs include clinginess, high emotional responsiveness, and hypersensitivity to any signs of rejection.[3] It's like wearing emotional radar glasses that detect the slightest emotional distance. So, someone who cherishes their independence might still be unable to stop feeling anxious in a relationship. When their partner spends time with friends or needs space, their emotional radar will blare at the highest decibels.

"Does this mean he doesn't care about me anymore?"

"Will she find someone better?"

Emotionally disabling thoughts like this will become prodding companions and likely compel this person to seek reassurance constantly.

People frequently misconstrue anxious attachment as mere neediness or clinginess, yet it has far-reaching consequences for emotional well-being and relationships. It's like comparing a sprinkle of salt to an ocean of emotions.

Renowned psychologist John Bowlby[4] introduced attachment theory in the 1950s, providing valuable insights into anxious attachment. Whether secure or inconsistent, our early interactions with caregivers shape our attachment style. For those with anxious attachments, the fear of abandonment becomes an ever-present shadow.

The science behind attachment theory offers hope and understanding for those on the path to healing. Research supports it: With self-awareness, therapy, and compassionate support, those with anxious attachment patterns can learn to develop more secure attachments.[5] This chapter opens that dialogue to help you gather what you need to understand what anxious attachment is, how it came to be in your life, how it impacts your relationships, and what you can do to eventually turn the emotional tide to a more secure attachment style.

The Birth of Anxious Attachment: Its Development from Childhood

Childhood, a time of innocence and wonder, is also the seedbed for the roots of our attachment styles. Picture young Timmy, wide-eyed and curious, reaching out to his mother for comfort after a little scrape on his knee. Sometimes, she wraps him in a warm embrace, soothing his pain and whispering comforting words. Other times, though, she's preoccupied with worries, barely sparing him a glance. Little does Timmy know that these seemingly insignificant moments lay the foundation for his anxious attachment style.

Bowlby's attachment theory states that children who experience inconsistent caregiver responses may develop an anxious attachment style.[6] It's like trying to find your way in a maze without a map—sometimes you receive warmth and love, and other times you're left to navigate the emotional labyrinth alone.

Anxious attachment doesn't always point to "bad" childhoods or neglectful parents. Attachment styles are as complex as a Rubik's cube, influenced by numerous factors. Even the best-intentioned parents can unknowingly contribute to their child's anxious attachment style. While early experiences of perceived abandonment or neglect can imprint within you, shaping your beliefs about yourself and others, the past does not define your future.

Let's peek into Maria's life as a woman in her 20s who recently discovered the origins of her anxious attachment style. A childhood memory unfolds—standing by the school gate, eagerly waiting for her parents to pick her up. Minutes turned into hours, and the echoes of other kids' laughter faded away as she felt left behind. This experience left her with a gnawing fear of being forgotten and unloved, yet now she's on a journey of healing. By shedding light on these experiences and understanding their impact, she is proactively rewriting her story and how she relates to others.

I invite you to do the same thing. Take a moment to wander through the corridors of your past. Can you recall specific instances from your childhood that may have contributed to your anxious attachment style? Embrace those memories gently, like holding a fragile butterfly in your hands. Remember, they do not define you; they are just stepping stones on your path to growth and transformation.

Taking It a Step Further: Exploring the Roots of Fear and Anxiety

Sigmund Freud was an Austrian neurologist and the founder of psychoanalysis, a groundbreaking approach to understanding the human mind and behavior. He believed our thoughts were like hidden treasure chests waiting to be unlocked, and he was right! According to his grand psychoanalytic theory, our minds house three essential aspects - the ego, id, and superego - each with unique characteristics.[7]

Think of the id as a restless kid seeking instant gratification, while the superego acts more like a strict teacher enforcing rules. Freud theorized that this mental dynamic develops through interactions with the world, societal influences, and the expectations of our parents. Meanwhile, the ego is the mental mediator, balancing the id's impulses and the superego's ideals. Its role is to find practical ways to satisfy desires while keeping things socially acceptable.

The ego acts as a mask, donned both online and offline. It's the voice that murmurs, "You must be more successful, more attractive, and more [insert societal standard] to be truly cherished." But imagine, for a breath, discarding that mask and glimpsing the vulnerable, imperfect, and profoundly beautiful core beneath it all.

Don't get me wrong—the ego isn't necessarily the villain of this story. Instead, it's trying to protect us from rejection and disappointment. Unfortunately, it's simultaneously leading us astray with its illusions. It's a well-intentioned but overzealous guardian, constantly looking for threats to our self-worth and security. And when it encounters anxious attachment, things can get quite interesting.

When the ego spots the vulnerability of anxious attachment, it jumps into action. It weaves stories of inadequacy, self-doubt, and unworthiness, whispering in our ears, "They're going to leave you" or "You're not lovable enough." The ego's programming runs deep, and in the realm of anxious attachment, it can lead to a pattern of seeking constant validation and reassurance from our partners. We become bounty hunters, constantly searching for that elusive affirmation that we are lovable and worthy of love. But no external consolation can fully quench the ego's thirst for security.

The only way to combat this is to embrace the understanding that you are not the ego. A practical way to make that separation is to give your ego a funny name. Can you imagine this? You and your partner sit in a cozy corner, sipping hot cocoa on a cold night. Cuddles are shared aplenty! Then, a worrisome thought sneaks in, trying to destroy this joyous mood. Don't let it. Be conscious of the fact that this is your ego talking. Don't try to hide it, either. Get your partner on your journey by sharing this playful practice of naming the ego. It's like having a secret code between you—an inside joke that reveals the ego for what it truly is—a mischievous little troublemaker. So, give that ego a funny name, like "Professor Worrypants" or "Madame Overthinker." As you giggle together, you'll both start to see that the ego is merely a character, not the show's main star.

Anxiety is a sneaky companion that likes to tag along with the ego. After all, they are both trying to protect us. When we experience anxiety, it's often a signal that our ego perceives a potential threat to our identity.

The ego doesn't like uncertainty. It prefers to operate within the boundaries of familiarity and control. In a way, anxiety is the ego's way of maintaining power by attempting to predict and manage potential dangers or adverse outcomes. When anxious thoughts arise, the ego tends to amplify them, making them feel more significant and tangible. It's like a skilled storyteller weaving elaborate tales of worst-case scenarios and "what ifs." In this process, the ego reinforces the belief that the thoughts directly reflect our identity and worth.

Awareness of this symbiotic relationship between anxiety and the ego is a game-changer. We untangle ourselves from the ego's clutches when we step into the observer role. By recognizing that anxious thoughts are not our thoughts but the ego's, we loosen the grip of the ego's programming.

In moments of anxiety, pause and take a breath. Ask yourself, "Is this thought a reflection of my true self, or is it just the ego's protective mechanism at play?"

Challenging the validity of anxious thoughts allows you to reclaim your power as the observer of your mind (you know, the real you). You will ultimately realize that anxiety and fear are not the architects of your relationships; they are just constructions of the ego. Sure, they try to take center stage, but deep down, you know that love thrives in an environment of trust, vulnerability, and open-heartedness.

So, I extend this invitation to you: Sit in the director's chair and watch the ego's antics unfold with a curious smile. Observe the anxious thoughts that come and go like clouds in the sky, knowing they do not define you. Becoming the master of your mind, no longer swayed by the ego's tricks.

As you journey toward this understanding, remember that it's a practice—a dance of self-discovery and self-compassion. And in this dance, you are not alone. Your partner in this adventure is your authentic self—the essence beyond the ego's facade.

Action Steps

Take a few minutes to sit comfortably and grab a notebook. Give a name to the egoic mind. Then, imagine you're a neutral observer, someone detached from your current thoughts. Begin writing down your reviews as if you're transcribing a conversation between two people—the "thinker" (ego) and the "observer" (the detached version of you). This exercise helps you gain distance from your thoughts, allowing you to view them more objectively. As you write, notice how your thoughts evolve, repeat, or change in tone, and consider how this new perspective impacts your understanding of your thought patterns.

Next, consider things from the perspective of your ego. You can start by addressing yourself in the following way:

Dear (Your Name),

I (Ego Name) am concerned about _________ and I think _________.

Just like before, let the thoughts flow unobstructed.

Step back into the role of the observer and look at this journal entry objectively. Ask yourself: Is it true? Are you 100% certain it's true? Who would you be without the thought? Who are you with the thought? Byron Katie's Four Questions inspire this introspective exercise and can help you gain insight into the ego's beliefs and judgments.[8]

Furthermore, consider practicing dialogues between your ego (the thinker) and your higher self (the inner therapist) in your journal entries. This exploration allows you to view situations from both perspectives and, as the observer, make decisions based on a more balanced understanding.

The Ripple Effect: How Anxious Attachment Impacts Relationships

Imagine you're by a tranquil lake. Its surface is still. When you drop a pebble into the water, ripples spread outward in widening circles. These ripples are akin to the influence of anxious attachment in a relationship, generating waves of tension and doubt. Recall times when you've felt clingy or sought constant reassurance from your partner—that's anxious attachment in motion. It's a subtle longing for security, creating disturbances like uncertainty and concern within the waters of your connection.

Just as those water ripples affect the entire lake, anxious attachment can influence the dynamics of your relationship. When you constantly seek reassurance and validation, your partner may feel like they're navigating a stormy sea of emotions. They might pull back, needing a little breathing room, leaving you even more anxious. It's like a cycle of waves, with each ripple reacting to the one before, creating a dance of emotions that can sometimes be overwhelming.

Take Raj, for instance. Of Indian ethnicity, he is a 40-year-old divorcee, always looking for signs of approval from his partners. Research by Feeney & Noller[9] reveals that many folks, just like Raj, have this nagging need for reassurance, and you know what's behind it? It's similar to the fear of being ghosted by someone you care about—the fear of abandonment! It's like a phantom is haunting Raj's thoughts, making him wonder, "What if she leaves me? Am I good enough? Does she genuinely love me?"

The need for reassurance can inadvertently create a self-fulfilling prophecy of rejection.[10] It's like a cosmic boomerang - we fear abandonment, seek relief to avoid it, and, in doing so, unintentionally push our partners away. But here's the thing - just as the ripples in the water eventually settle, so too can the anxious attachment in your relationship. By recognizing these patterns and understanding the roots of your anxieties, you can become like a skilled sailor, navigating these waters with greater ease.

Let's discuss these patterns now:

Communication Challenges

Anxious attachment can be a roadblock placed smack dab in the middle of effective relationship communication. You know those moments when you have something on your mind and heart to say, but a little voice whispers, "What if they don't get it? What if it causes a big argument?" The internal battle feels like balancing a tightrope between saying what you think and avoiding potential conflict.

Salma is right in the middle of this communication tightrope act. When she needs to express her concerns or frustrations to her partner, she fears it might rock the boat, making him withdraw or upset. So, she ends up bottling up her feelings and keeping them locked away. But as time passes, the unspoken words pile up, creating a rift between them, like a wall slowly rising between two hearts.

Overthinking and Hyper-Vigilance

Being anxiously attached means that, likely, there are times when every little word, gesture, or action from your partner feels like a secret code you're trying to crack. We can't help but pull out our detective's magnifying glass, constantly searching for hidden meanings in every move they make. Sherlock Holmes has nothing on us when we look for signs of dissatisfaction or impending abandonment. So, we find ourselves in a whirlwind of self-monitoring. Yet, the thing is that this never-ending analysis leads to a merry-go-round of anxiety, spinning us in circles and perpetuating our worries.

Anxious attachment tendencies don't only show up in romantic relationships. No relationship is exempt, a fact that Reggie knows all too well. He is right in the thick of this overthinking adventure. He has always felt like his parents' least favorite of his siblings. His anxious attachment style has him on high alert, scanning for any signs to verify if his assumption is valid. It's like he's got a mental supercomputer analyzing every interaction with his parents. But here's the twist - this overthinking "superpower" doesn't come without a cost. Reggie feels mentally drained and unable to fully enjoy the precious moments of the present when the family gathers.

Relationship Insecurity

In exploring anxious attachment, it's hard not to encounter the profound insecurity that permeates relationships. This lack of security manifests as the gnawing fear of abandonment or rejection, which can turn our minds into overactive detectives, seeking evidence of our partner's feelings even when everything seems fine. This constant doubting robs us of the sheer joy and presence we deserve in our relationships, leaving us stuck in a cycle of unease.

Lina Kim is a determined tech entrepreneur from Seoul, South Korea. She is known for her innovative solutions in the field of sustainable energy. She is the last person anyone would suspect of suffering from a case of being insecure in her relationship. Yet that friend who's constantly texting their partner for constant reminders of love and loyalty? That's her! But underneath her search for certainty lies a sea of doubts and insecurities, making her relationship a bit like a rollercoaster ride with more tension than thrills.

It doesn't end there. We might unintentionally become control freaks when anxious about losing someone we care about. We start trying to micromanage every aspect of the relationship, thinking it'll somehow quell our fears. Yet, in reality, it just adds more complications and challenges. Been there, done that, right?

Intense Need for Reassurance

Individuals with an anxious attachment style have a hunger for reassurance that's as relentless as a swarm of bees buzzing around honey. It can feel like they're on a never-ending quest to find evidence of their partner's love and commitment, hoping it'll be the magic potion to silence their fear of being left in the lurch.

Take Emily, for instance—she's the ultimate reassurance seeker! If her best friend doesn't reply to a text immediately or dares to disagree, her mind will instantly go into overdrive, conjuring thoughts of abandonment. Anxiously, she'll pester her with questions, seeking that all-important affirmation that she is her favorite and only best friend. But this constant craving for validation became a heavy load on their relationship, suffocating her friend, who felt she couldn't keep up with this unquenchable thirst for reassurance.

Jealousy and Possessiveness

An anxious attachment style often leads to feeling jealous and possessive in relationships, as the anxious attacher incessantly compares themselves to others and fears they might be replaced or abandoned at any moment. This fear can unleash a whirlwind of controlling behaviors, where they snoop around and monitor their partner's every move.

The epitome of an anxious attachment warrior is Alex. Whenever his partner interacts with anyone of the opposite sex, his mind transforms into a bustling marketplace of doubts, where worst-case scenarios sell like hotcakes. His insecurities lead him down the dark path of possessive behaviors, which act like an avalanche, burying trust and freedom in their relationship.

Emotional Rollercoasters

Let's step into the rollercoaster world of anxious attachment and buckle up for a ride filled with emotional highs and lows. I bet it feels like being on cloud nine when your partner showers you with attention and affection—pure bliss! You feel like you are floating in the air, your heart dancing with joy. But hold on tight because those euphoric feelings can come crashing down in the blink of an eye, sending you into a tailspin of anxiety and despair. It's a see-saw of emotions, with every gesture from your partner becoming a potential trigger for a whirlwind of doubts and fears. These fluctuations create instability and emotional strain in your relationship, conditions not conducive for continued bliss.

Meet our protagonist, Chris—the quintessential anxious attachment aficionado! When his partner, José, is all lovey-dovey and attentive, Chris's heart soars like a majestic eagle in the sky. But as life gets in the way and his partner becomes busy, his mind transforms into a tangled web of worries. He starts questioning his love and dedication, assuming their distance means José's about to abandon ship. Here comes the emotional turmoil and the endless pursuit of reassurance, leaving poor Chris trapped in a cycle of craving validation for his ongoing affection toward him.

Codependency Tendencies

Those with this attachment style tend to have an insatiable craving for approval and validation from others. The opinions of others become the measuring stick for their self-worth. And the catch is this need for validation can lead them to put their partner's needs on a pedestal, forgetting to take care of their emotional hunger. This is codependency, a psychological condition where a person becomes overly reliant on another, often at the expense of their well-being.[11] It involves an unhealthy pattern of enabling and caretaking, leading to difficulties in establishing healthy boundaries and fostering an unhealthy reliance on the other person for emotional validation and fulfillment.

Emma is codependent in her romantic relationships. She constantly seeks her partner's approval, using their opinions as a compass to navigate her life. Make decisions independently? Inconceivable! She fears being alone so much that she will go to great lengths to keep the relationship intact, even if it means sacrificing her needs.

Struggle to Trust

In the recipe for a healthy relationship, trust is the secret ingredient that makes it all come together. But for those with anxious attachments, this essential ingredient seems to hide in the shadows, playing hard to get. They're on guard, shielding themselves from potential heartache, all because of deep-rooted insecurities and past betrayals that have left their hearts scarred. Trust becomes an elusive butterfly, flitting just out of reach, leaving them skeptical and preventing them from wholeheartedly believing in their partner's love and loyalty.

Camilla's longing for trust at work is hindered by her history of professional disappointments and lingering self-doubt; she wears an armor of skepticism, shielding herself from potential letdowns and creating a barrier to the collaborative connections she yearns for.

Do any of these examples resonate with you? Are you tangled in the web of anxious attachment in your relationships? Experiencing the effects of anxious attachment in your relationship is distressing and disruptive, but here's the silver lining: You have the incredible power to break free from these patterns and find the road to healthier, more secure connections.

Start by keeping these effects in mind. Here's a fun little trick to help you navigate the signs of anxious attachment like a pro. Say hello to the acronym C.H.I.R. J.E.C.T. – it sounds like "Sure, Ject" (I know, it's weirdly amusing!). It stands for:

- **C** = Communication Challenges
- **H** = Hyper-Vigilance & Overthinking
- **I** = Insecurities
- **R** = Intense Need for Reassurance
- **J** = Jealousy and Possessiveness
- **E** = Emotional Rollercoaster
- **C** = Codependency
- **T** = Struggles to Trust

This magical reminder is your secret weapon, pointing out the signs of anxious attachment as they appear. Naming it is the key to taming it! The moment you become aware of any CHIRJECT signs, their power over you starts to crumble, and you become one step closer to embracing the secure attachment style you deserve.

Do you remember reciting poems in kindergarten and preschool? Those are some of the most nostalgic memories of our childhood, but they were for more than just fun. Reciting poems helps kids learn.[12] The fantastic benefits do not disappear once we reach the legal age to consume alcohol. Reciting a poem still helps adults retain information and rewire their brains for better living. 13

Make awareness of these potential pitfalls in your relationship easier to remember by memorizing this poem:

C is for communication, challenges we face,
H reminds us of Hyper-Vigilance, a relentless chase.
I stand for Insecurities lurking in our minds.
R represents the Intense Need for Reassurance we find.
J is for Jealousy and Possessiveness, a battle within.
E brings the Emotional Rollercoaster, where emotions spin.
C signifies codependency, entangled we may be.
T reminds us of Struggles to Trust, a journey we must see.
Remember "CHIRJECT" in times of need.
To understand anxious attachment's seed.

With this poem in your heart and mind, set sail on a journey to decipher the signs, leaving worries behind. "CHIRJECT" is your guide to conquering anxious attachment's tide, like a brave sailor navigating stormy waters.

But hey, it's not all doom and gloom! Bright skies are ahead. Understanding and embracing your anxious attachment style is the first step toward healing and building healthier relationships.

Action Steps

Learn the acronym and poem above. Make it enjoyable by humming it throughout the day, even if it feels silly. This simple practice can bring a lighthearted touch to self-awareness and ground you in times when you recognize that you are displaying these signs. Need help remembering things? Not to worry, handy dandy Post-it notes to the rescue! Grab a Post-it note and write down the acronym and poem. Then, stick the Post-it note somewhere, like in your bathroom mirror or car dashboard, so you can look at it occasionally.

Realizing Your Attachment Style is Not Your Identity

Imagine your identity as the colorful and intricate puzzle that makes you, well, you! It's like a unique combination of all the little pieces that come together to form your personality, your beliefs, and your life experiences. It makes you stand out in a crowd and feel like the unique individual you are. Anxious attachment is not one of these puzzle pieces.

Rather than having a fixed identity, think of attachment styles as trying on different hats! Sometimes, you wear the "Anxious Attachment" hat, and other times, you might slip on the "Secure Attachment" hat. It's like having a collection of hats; we all have a little bit of each attachment style tucked away in our closets.

So, let's do a fun wardrobe assessment - what's the percentage of each attachment style you have? Maybe you're 40% "Anxious Attachment," 30% "Secure Attachment," and 30% "Avoidant Attachment." Embrace your hat collection's diversity, knowing it's not set in stone.

The secret sauce to cultivating a secure attachment style is to remove the label "I am An Anxiously Attached Person" and replace it with "I have portrayed signs of Anxious Attachment, but that is not who I am." Commit to changing those labels, like rearranging your wardrobe, and watch how it transforms your self-identification.

Let's do this powerful exercise together: pledge to revamp your mental wardrobe—trade old hats for new ones that fit better and suit you perfectly. Step by step, embrace the power of possibility, knowing you can build a stronger foundation of secure attachment, one hat at a time. Toss away limiting labels, embrace the diversity of your attachment styles, and embark on this transformative adventure of healing and growth. You've got this!

Decoding Your Emotional GPS

∞

They say we're not just the sum of our thoughts, words, or feelings; rather, it is the choices we make and the behaviors we repeat that define us. Over time, these actions harden into habits, shaping the essence of our character and carving the path to our ultimate destiny. Unquestionably, our actions motivate us as people; they are the compass that directs us through chaos.

But where do our emotions fit in amidst the hustle and bustle of the rat race and all the other paths in this life journey? How do they sway the tides of what we do? How do they affect our interactions with others? Each emotion we experience holds profound significance. Guilt is a moral wake-up call, while anger shows us what we are attached to. Love warmly assures us we are cherished, worthy, and safe—simply for being ourselves.

Picture these emotions as your GPS, lighting the way through life's winding roads. Like a seasoned navigator, each emotion marks your starting point—a beacon of where you stand. Whether you're bathed in sadness, dancing with joy, engulfed in fear, lost in loneliness, beaming with pride, or walking tall confidently, these emotions sketch the map of your journey. They guide you, telling you what to do and where to go.

They do not define you, but instead, they point the way. Fear, for instance, can catalyze you to pursue peace and safety. You can realize this possibility by allowing this emotion to ignite your internal GPS and chart the most promising course to your sanctuary. You are the driver of this odyssey, not anxiety or any other feeling. The GPS may guide you, but the final destination rests in your hands.

No, there's no high-tech shortcut here; you must navigate the old-fashioned way—by drawing out the daily steps that lead to your desired horizon. This chapter helps you recalibrate your emotional GPS to chart a course toward healing, self-discovery, and growth.

The Tug of Anxiety: Recognizing Fear of Abandonment

Consider a little girl named Krissy, an only child from Australia. Her parents were dedicated professionals in fast-paced careers looking to make a name for themselves and leave a mark on the world. While they loved

Krissy deeply, they didn't always have the time or emotional availability to be there for her consistently. Sometimes, they were warm and affectionate; other times, they seemed distant and preoccupied with meetings, deadlines, and demanding bosses. Krissy remembers frequently waiting for her parents to give her a good night kiss but only being met with birds chirping to awaken the new day when they spent the night at the office.

As a result, Krissy developed an anxious attachment style, and a little voice inside her head constantly whispered, "What if they never come back? Will they always be there for me?" This fear of abandonment lingered into her adulthood and influenced her relationships.

In one of Krissy's romantic relationships, she met Eli, a caring and loving partner. But Krissy's anxiety kicked in whenever Eli spent time away from her for work or other commitments. She'd start worrying if he still cared for her or would eventually leave her. This fear made her constantly seek reassurance from Eli, seeking texts or calls to feel secure.

One day, after Eli returned from a work trip, Krissy couldn't help but ask him, "Are you sure everything is okay between us?" Eli hugged her gently, saying, "I understand your fear and want you to know I care deeply about you. We can trust each other. I'm here for you, even when we're apart. We can work through any challenges together."

Through Eli's reassuring words and consistent support, Krissy began feeling slightly more at ease. However, her fear of abandonment didn't vanish overnight. It was like a well-worn path in her mind that needed time and patience to change.

Krissy decided to explore her fear further. She reflected on her childhood experiences and realized how her parents' inconsistency had shaped her attachment style. It also affected other areas of her life, like her workplace relationships and friendships. She often found herself calling up her friends to confirm their plans, even though they did not show signs that they would ditch her at the last minute, and she was not committing to doing her best at work because she did not want to be like her parents. She acknowledged that her fear was a signal, calling her to heal the wounds of the past and build a stronger sense of security within herself.

As Krissy opened up to Eli about her journey of self-discovery, he shared some of his vulnerabilities. Eli admitted that he also had his insecurities and fears, and they decided to be each other's support system. Together, they created a safe space for vulnerability and growth.

Krissy learned that her fear of abandonment was not a flaw but a part of her story. It was a sign that she craved emotional connection and closeness in her relationships. Embracing this truth allowed her to communicate her needs more openly with Eli and helped him understand her on a deeper level.

With time and effort, Krissy's fear of being abandoned began to loosen its grip on her heart. It didn't vanish entirely, but she learned to recognize it as a signal, guiding her to seek comfort, love, and reassurance when needed. Krissy gradually reprogrammed her emotional GPS through self-compassion, steering her toward a more secure attachment style.

Our experiences in the past have shaped the emotional baggage that each of us carries, as Krissy's journey demonstrates. By acknowledging our fears, sharing our vulnerabilities, and offering understanding and support to one another, we can navigate the complexities of attachment and create more robust, more fulfilling relationships. It's a journey worth taking, leading us to a place of deeper connection and love.

Do you also experience the fear of abandonment like Krissy does? Instead of being guided by this fear, use it for what it truly is—a powerful emotional signal.[14] It tells you that you have a strong need for emotional connection and closeness with your partner or loved ones. This fear may be a protective mechanism, urging you to seek proximity and emotional responsiveness from others to feel secure and validated in the relationship.

This fear is an alarm system alerting you to potential threats to your emotional bonds. It can signal a desire for deeper emotional intimacy, reassurance, support, or even a call to address underlying insecurities and unresolved attachment issues. Recognizing and understanding this fear can be a starting point for you to explore your attachment patterns, heal past wounds, and cultivate healthier and more secure relationships. By acknowledging and working through this fear, you can gradually build trust, develop stronger emotional connections, and move toward a more secure attachment style.

Journal Prompts

Using a journal can be a powerful tool. It provides a safe space to express and reflect on your feelings, fears, and thought patterns. Writing down your thoughts helps you gain clarity, identify triggers, and develop healthier perspectives, ultimately fostering self-awareness and promoting emotional growth. As such, journal questions and prompts are throughout these chapters. Answer these questions honestly and with as much expression as you can muster. Remember, your journal is a safe space.

To start, here are a few questions to help you identify any signs that you have a fear of abandonment:

- When have I felt a heightened sense of fear or insecurity in my relationships, and what were the specific circumstances surrounding those feelings?

- Are there any recurring patterns in my thoughts or behaviors that indicate I might be experiencing a fear of abandonment?
- How do I react when a loved one spends time apart from me? What emotions arise, and why?

The Cling and Distance Dance: Understanding Anxious Behaviors

Let's say you've found yourself in the embrace of a truly loving and supportive partner. All should be going well, but it isn't. A haunting fear of rejection still lingers, casting a shadow over the beauty of your relationship. It becomes a tug-of-war between the rational part that knows how wonderful your partner treats you and the persistent, louder voice that whispers about potential hurt.

If this rings true for you, it's a strong signal that echoes of past relationships are reverberating within you. Even when your mind acknowledges your partner's commitment and affection, your body is flooded with anxiety and dread at the thought of heartbreak. You might catch yourself dissecting every word your partner utters, analyzing each fleeting expression in their eyes. Hours later, lost in the maze of thoughts, you realize your shoulders have crept up toward your ears, tension gripping your body like a vice.

It isn't your fault because the aftermath of unresolved trauma, whether a single harrowing event or the slow erosion of daily stressors, has taken residence in your body. Being hurt by a past relationship is an example of such trauma.

Our bodies are finely tuned instruments designed to adapt and protect us. In response to trauma, they can engage in a remarkable act of self-preservation by locking away these painful experiences. Even when it is not the foremost thing on your mind, the body remembers the ordeals you survived, resulting in physical tension, chronic pain, and emotional distress. Like an old, ghostly resonance, trauma amplifies your fear of rejection even when there's no genuine threat.

This doesn't reflect your character; it doesn't mean you are broken. Trauma leaves its mark deep within, sparking irrational fears within your nervous system and brain.[15] Even if decades have passed since that trauma, the past's specter looms over the present, its intensity almost as vivid as the initial experience itself.

Mike is a 40-year-old man freshly navigating the terrain of post-divorce life after a rocky marriage. In his new relationship, Mike craves the warmth of intimacy with his girlfriend yet recoils at the thought of getting too close. He keeps swinging between moments of overwhelming affection and sudden emotional distance. Whenever he pendulums toward emotional distance, he habitually grinds his teeth.

Dissecting his behaviors, you'll find they are rooted in a primal fear—the fear of being cast aside and rejected by the person he's drawn to. This fear turns Mike's relationship into a cycle of high moments of connection and clinging and dips of detachment. These highs and lows create a whirlwind of instability that bewilders him and his partner.

Mike's fear triggers responses that might seem puzzling at first. He might struggle to trust, doubting the authenticity of his partner's feelings. He might become a martyr, bending backward to please in hopes of avoiding rejection—a behavior known as "fawning."[16] And then there's the unquenchable thirst for reassurance, an insatiable need for his partner to affirm her affections repeatedly.

Escaping this never-ending loop takes two steps. The first step is all about noticing. More aptly, it is about being mindful of what you think, feel, and, thus, do. Being more mindful, Mike goes through this cycle by thinking he will be abandoned, feeling fear, and then pulling away, manifesting in his body as teeth grinding. Do you get super close and back out suddenly, just like Mike? This awareness allows you to spot patterns in how you act in relationships.

Mindfulness, the practice of being fully present in the moment without judgment, is the second step. It offers a key to unlocking the vault of stored trauma in our bodies. It acts as a bridge between our conscious awareness and the buried trauma. The practice turns our attention inward, making us keenly aware of our sensations, thoughts, and emotions. In doing so, we notice our bodies' subtle signals—tension in the shoulders, a racing heartbeat, or a clenched jaw. In Mike's case, it is teeth-grinding. These are the body's whispers, indicators of where trauma may be stored.

Mindfulness invites us to approach these sensations with compassion rather than avoidance. As we acknowledge the discomfort, we create a safe space for our bodies to release the trauma they have held. It's a gradual process that requires patience and self-acceptance. With continued practice, we learn to breathe into the areas of tension, allowing them to soften and unravel. This release accompanies a flood of emotions—grief, anger, or fear—that have long been suppressed. Mindfulness grants us the strength to confront these emotions without judgment, allowing them to flow and ultimately dissipate.

Moreover, mindfulness helps us to rewrite our relationship with our past. Instead of being imprisoned by our trauma, we gain a sense of empowerment and control. We can reshape our narrative by integrating the lessons learned from our painful experiences into our growth and resilience.

Mindfulness is truly a superpower because it transforms the way your body responds. It goes from that edgy, anxious state caused by fear to a more relaxed and balanced mode.[17] Mindfulness helps your body and brain chill out so you are more in control of how you react to your feelings.

Meditation strengthens the foundation of mindfulness. When the mind often spirals into overthinking and negativity, meditation becomes the anchor that steadies our mental ship. We deliberately hone our awareness through meditation and gently guide our wandering thoughts to the present moment. By learning to observe our thoughts without judgment during meditation, we break free from the grip of anxious rumination, allowing us to rewrite the narratives that keep us tethered to insecurity.

Knowing is just the beginning. It would be best to act differently to change how anxiety affects your relationships. It's like learning a new dance routine to replace old steps. Instead of letting fear call the shots, you start practicing new behaviors that feel better to you and your partner.

So, picture Mike again, armed with mindfulness. He takes a moment when he gets the urge to shower his partner with affection or pull away. During this pause, he chooses a different response that matches what he's learned about attachment patterns. He's rewriting the dance steps in the middle of the song. Moreover, heightened self-awareness enables him to recognize teeth grinding, a largely unconscious behavior. When he feels the urge, he can delve into his inner thoughts and emotions, discerning how they manifest in his actions and behavior.

To sum it all up, breaking free from this cycle that develops due to the fear of rejection is like learning a dance with two parts: understanding the patterns that fear sets up and then using mindfulness to pick new steps to improve the dance. It's about changing how you react and becoming more intentional. This dance becomes smoother with time, and your relationships become more meaningful and healing.

Action Steps

Follow the steps of this mindful meditation exercise to become more in tune with any fear of rejection you harbor:

- Find a quiet and comfortable place to sit or lie down.

- Close your eyes and take a few deep breaths to relax. Allow your awareness to settle into your body.

- Imagine a clear blue sky in your mind.
- Begin with a body scan, slowly moving your attention from the top of your head to your toes. Notice any areas of tension or discomfort.
- Now, visualize a thought cloud drifting by in that sky.
- With each inhale, acknowledge a fear or thought related to rejection that comes to your mind. Let your breath be a soothing anchor.
- As you exhale, imagine that thought being gently captured by the thought cloud and floating away, all while keeping your awareness on your body.
- Keep repeating this process, allowing thoughts about rejection to arise and releasing them with each exhale. Continue to scan your body for any sensations.
- Notice how the thought clouds come and go, just like passing thoughts. Your body may also respond and release tension as you do this.
- Whenever you get caught up in a particular thought or sensation, gently bring your focus

back to the thought clouds and your breath while also staying aware of your body's feelings.

- After a few minutes, when you're ready, open your eyes and take a moment to ground yourself in the present moment, fully aware of your thoughts and the sensations in your body.

Excessive Sensitivity to Relationship Dynamics

Our anxieties can magnify our emotional responses. Anxious individuals often harbor a heightened fear of abandonment or rejection, making them hyper-vigilant in their relationships. This hyper-vigilance manifests as hypersensitivity.

Hypersensitivity is excessively or extremely sensitive to stimuli like situations and emotions.[18] Anxious attachment and being hyper-sensitive go together like peanut butter and jelly (but are not nearly as tasty). Have you ever found yourself exceptionally attuned to even the slightest shift in mood, tone, or behavior of your partner, noticing nuances that most people would overlook? This heightened sensitivity can lead you down a rabbit hole of overthinking, where you try to read between the lines of your partner's words and gestures.

Laura, a 25-year-old from Denmark, is caught in this web of over-analysis. She's in a relationship with a guy she genuinely cares about and who she thinks cares about her, but every time he 'ignores' a text or even raises an eyebrow, her mind goes into overdrive. She dissects every syllable, searching for clues, signs that rejection or abandonment loom on the horizon of their relationship.

She often rides high on the thrill of affection with her boyfriend, only to find herself plummeting into the abyss of doubt and anxiety the next. This has led this relationship down a rocky road where tension runs high, and conflict is inevitable. Laura, already on high alert, often misinterprets a casual comment from her boyfriend as a sign that he's pulling away. This tiny spark ignites a whole firestorm of emotions, leading to arguments that might have never happened without her finely-tuned radar for emotional subtleties.

And therein lies the challenge. Learning to differentiate between real issues and those that exist only in the realm of perception is a journey fraught with twists and turns. Dealing with anxious attachment means grappling with self-doubt, where every interaction becomes a puzzle to solve and every word a potential clue to decode. But we must learn that not every raised eyebrow means something significant. Not every pause in conversation is a harbinger of doom.

So, whether you're Laura or someone who can relate to her journey, the key lies in finding that balance. It's about acknowledging your sensitivity and ability to tune into the subtleties while understanding that not everything requires intense scrutiny. Accept that relationships are complex, dynamic, and sometimes messy; they don't fit neatly into prediction boxes.

Be kind to yourself if you deal with hypersensitivity. Remind yourself that your hyper-awareness is a trait that can be both a gift and a challenge. Learning to discern between what's real and what's perceived is a skill that, with time and practice, can lead to more peaceful relationships built on trust and understanding.

Journal Prompt

In your journal, describe how you react when you perceive a slight criticism from a loved one. Be specific. What physical sensations, thoughts, or emotions arise in those moments?

The Craving for Constant Reassurance: Seeking Validation

Have you ever found yourself in self-doubt, questioning every move you make? And who hasn't had that fear of saying or doing something that could potentially jeopardize a relationship they cherish? We all seek that reassurance—that we're on the right track, that we matter, and that our connections are secure. Even if you're the most confident person out there, there are times when those doubts creep in. It's human nature.[19] Seeking a little validation and reassurance is like a gentle nudge to your heart, letting you know you're not alone in these thoughts.

But, like with anything, there's a balance. Seeking reassurance is entirely okay. However, if you find yourself *constantly* seeking assurance, there is something more beneath the surface.

Andre has found it hard to find that balance. This 33-year-old man grapples with a relentless need for reassurance from his partner. He keeps asking for affirmations of her devotion, looking for that magic reassurance to silence his worries forever.

A paradox arises, though. The more Andre seeks reassurance, the more it inadvertently strains the relationships he's trying to protect. No matter how understanding, partners can be opposed to repeatedly asking the same question. It's like a song stuck on replay; with time, it can lead to emotional exhaustion and resentment. It's not that they don't care - it's just that the constant reassurance-seeking can feel like an unending demand they're struggling to meet.

But even within this irony, there's a path to healing. It starts with learning to find solace within yourself, which means being your source of comfort at times. Being able to comfort yourself is like having a toolkit of emotional first aid – you're the one who knows best how to mend those emotional bruises. Self-soothing brings you to the understanding that while reassurance from others can be a wonderful balm, the true power lies in being able to reassure yourself.

Action Steps

Create your own "Self-Reassurance Box" by finding a small container and collecting meaningful notes and reminders. Fill it with affirmations like "I am capable of handling challenges," heartfelt messages from friends and family, love notes from yourself, inspiring quotes, future self-notes, favorite memes - anything that brings you comfort and reassurance. When anxiety or stress creeps in, open your box and choose a note at random. Take a moment to absorb the positive message. This practice can help redirect your thoughts and provide a reassuring boost in moments of self-doubt or distress.

The Mirage of Perfection: Idealizing Partners

Have you ever seen someone—a friend, a partner, or even a celebrity—and you just thought they were the bee's knees like they can do no wrong? That's a taste of idealization [20] - a mental trick our brains play on us.

You know how some days you wake up feeling like a superhero, ready to conquer the world? Well, idealization is like putting someone else in that superhero cape, making them seem like they've got it all together with a dash of glitter and magic. It's your brain's way of turning up the brightness of someone's qualities and making their flaws practically invisible.

However, there is a hidden twist. Idealization is more than just picturing someone as the world's best human. It's actually a defense mechanism against anxiousness. Imagine you have a super fantastic friend, but you're worried they won't like you as much as you like them. Idealization comes to the rescue, painting them as the ideal friend who will never disappoint you.

It gets even more enjoyable. Sometimes, this superhero cape gets passed around like a hot potato. You might go from thinking your friend is the best thing since sliced bread to suddenly feeling like they're a villain in your story. This switcheroo is called devaluation,[21] where the same person you put on a pedestal becomes the target of your frustration.

Flipping the script like this doesn't just happen in friendships. It also occurs in romantic relationships. 28-year-old Maria has fallen into the trap of idealization repeatedly. To her, her partners can do no wrong. They're like these flawless beings she's fortunate enough to be with. The idealized image she holds them to is impossibly high, but reality inevitably clashes with the ideal. The heartbreak of disappointment rushes in, leaving her feeling betrayed by the very perfection she envisioned.

This cycle of idealization and disillusionment sets the stage for an unhealthy dynamic. It's like walking a tightrope of unrealistic expectations, where your partner's every move is measured against a lofty standard they never agreed to. This dance can overshadow your own needs and boundaries. You're so busy admiring their imagined perfection that you forget about your well-being.

But to foster healthy relationships, we need to see partners through a realistic lens by removing the rose-tinted glasses and seeing them for what they are. It's about acknowledging that, yes, they're lovely, but they're also human – with flaws, quirks, and imperfections that make them beautifully real. It's like accepting that a painting isn't just defined by its brightest strokes but also by the intricate shadows that give it depth. In relationships, embracing the entirety of your partner—their strengths and their weaknesses - allows you to build a connection based on genuine understanding.

Journal Prompts

Do you need to figure out if you idealize anyone in your life? Answer these journal questions to find out:

- When considering my relationships, do I often focus on the person's positive traits and ignore any negative aspects?
- Have I noticed a pattern of feeling disappointed or disillusioned when people don't meet my high expectations?
- How do I react when someone I admire makes a mistake or shows a flaw? Do I find it challenging to accept imperfections?
- Can I identify any past instances where I ignored red flags or warning signs because I fixated on an idealized image of the person?

Navigating the Storm

Coping with Anxiety in Anxious Attachment

∞

Anxiety and anxious attachment, like two sides of the same coin, frequently appear hand in hand. Anxiety is a natural defense mechanism.[22] It springs to life when we encounter situations lacking control or steeped in uncertainty. It stems from the fear of abandonment and the apprehension that our needs might go unmet, and it especially takes root with attachment.

Anxiety is not the adversary it's often made out to be. Instead, it's a messenger that directs your attention to an issue that needs resolution. While anxiety serves the purpose of safeguarding us, our genuine aspiration is to thrive. When anxiety's grip tightens, it's easy to feel overwhelmed and lost in the swirl of our thoughts. In these moments, pausing and trusting life's process is valuable. Reflect upon past experiences, recognizing that lessons emerge and beauty can flourish even amidst chaos. Surrendering to this process and embracing trust allows us to open ourselves to new prospects and genuinely appreciate life's changes.

In the context of romance, anxiety can manifest as an ongoing concern over your relationship status, especially prevalent among the community of people with an anxious attachment style. Take the example of Risa, who resides in a high-rise apartment in Chicago and is a 36-year-old single woman who constantly checks her phone for social media notifications. The compulsion is understandable; she's afraid of missing any interaction. However, this behavior stems from her attachment to social media validation. Her fixation on likes, comments, and messages stems from a deep need to be liked and followed, essentially seeking reassurance that she's not overlooked.

This habit might seem innocuous, but it shows her dependence on external validation for her self-worth. Risa's phone has become her security blanket; those notifications determine her emotional state. Regrettably, this cycle entangles her in a loop where she's perpetually seeking others' approval instead of cultivating self-assurance. The consequence? She loses her autonomy and confidence, tied to the whims of her notifications. The constant anticipation of messages leads her to overanalyze every word, turning simple interactions into complex puzzles as she searches for hidden meanings.

Can you see how anxiety can develop in such circumstances? Research conducted by Mikulincer and Shaver in 2007[23] found that "attachment anxiety is associated with increased negative emotional responses, heightened detection of threats in the environment, and negative views of the self." This emphasizes the seriousness of anxious attachment's impact on your emotional landscape. By understanding the intricate relationship between anxiety and attachment, you can foster greater self-awareness and ultimately work toward building healthier, more resilient connections. This chapter helps you take a step in that direction.

The Root of Anxiety in Anxious Attachment

Fear and anxiety, those powerful (and pesky) emotions we all know too well, have an uncanny ability to hold us captive, mess with our thoughts, and put hurdles in our path to personal growth. Have you ever taken a moment to ponder where these feelings come from? What roots do they have, and better yet, how can we shake off their hold and find our way to a brighter side?

The home of fear and anxiety is the ego, the complex web of how we see ourselves. It creates distinctions and decides what's "right" and "wrong." This mental factory creates all the labels, associations, and identities that fill our minds. Since this cognitive tool tries to make sense of the world around us, it sorts, labels, and gives meaning to everything it encounters. It takes on the roles of a historian, documenting our past experiences, and a guard, trying to keep us safe in the present. This is how it travels through our memories, altering how we see the world now, with the primary objective of assisting us in survival mode, even if it means we don't thrive.

The ego has been hanging around since we humans got the hang of language. When we started talking, we also sorted things into categories and gave them names. It's like when we say "bird." Instead of appreciating the unique beauty of each bird species, we just slapped them all with the "bird" label. And then we started thinking all birds could fly, even though penguins and ostriches didn't get that memo. It's funny how these labels can create false ideas, right? Our projections and ideas start getting tangled up in these labels, shifting our focus from what's in front of us.

Have you ever heard yourself saying, "Oh, it's another one of those birds I saw before," without looking closely? Yep, those labels mess with your perception. We see something unique as just another ordinary thing, like casually saying, "Oh, it's just another pigeon."

But the ego doesn't stop there; it swipes away the beauty around us and pulls us away from the present moment if we let it. It links what's happening now to what we understood before. That's why we start thinking, "Is he ignoring me? Is he cheating like my last partner did?" That is likely the ego's way of playing tricks on us.

Talking about labels, did you know that we humans slap labels on ourselves, too? Like with "birds," we get a name when we are born. The ego loves pretending our name or job title is who we are. It even gets us thinking we are our bodies, our personalities, and what others say about us.

The ego is a cheeky storyteller. It wants us to think we are our thoughts and that they're our reality. When we start believing that we're the body, the thoughts, and the personality, the ego tricks us into thinking that anything messing with these labels threatens our control of reality.

Let's break this down further because the ego has a way of masking itself as your gut feeling or even the real you when it is just basic programming installed when you were a kid learning language and labels. Think of it like apps on a phone—the phone itself isn't the notifications it sends. The same goes for us. We aren't the thoughts zinging around in our heads. If we were creating every thought, wouldn't we choose happier ones? We wouldn't pick anxiety and fear, right? We would not have thoughts like "I am afraid of losing her" taking up space in our heads. Those thoughts just pop up on their own.

How different would things be if you had that type of control? The great thing is that you do have power in this situation. You can internalize the fundamental truth:

you are not the ego. You're not producing those anxious thoughts or the fears that keep you awake at night. You're the spectator, watching these thoughts drift by. When you realize this, you set yourself up to break free from anxiety's grip.

Now, why does the ego play this trick on us? Why does it want us to believe that fear and anxiety are who we are? We have natural selection to thank for this "gift." Let's journey back to cave days—think of Beatrice and Bianca, two lovely cave ladies. Beatrice is all nervous, listening to monsters in the woods. Feelings of anxiety and fear make her more cautious. She listens to every sound, wondering if it's a potential danger. Also, her worried nature has forced her to learn techniques to survive an attack from a wild animal.

On the other hand, Bianca is carefree. With her cheerful nature, she walks through the forest without a care in the world, singing to herself and frolicking. She doesn't even pay attention to where she steps, much less think about what danger could lurk around the next tree.

Our ancestors' world was full of physical dangers, so who do you think would survive to see another day and make babies to pass on the human gene? Beatrice, anxious and fearful, survives, right? That's the ego at work, making sure we survive.

Over these thousands of years, we have nurtured the ego, but now it's time to unlearn this survival mode.

Unless you are like our tax accountant and realize, "I get paid to be paranoid," keep it up! Otherwise, you're doing great if you're reading this book.

How do you unlearn the programming that is wired into our DNA? Here's a playful trick from the Clarity Catalyst Coach certification program at Stanford University: [24] After you've given your ego a funny name, like "Mr. Worrywart" or "Mrs. Anxiety Pants," as we discussed earlier, take it a step further and draw it. Maybe it looks like a child, a monster, or a stick figure. That drawing? It's proof that your ego is separate from you. Share this with your partner for some lighthearted fun. This helps you see that anxious thoughts don't define you or your relationship.

Now, let's look at the intricate dance between anxiety and control. It's truly fascinating how we sometimes trick ourselves into thinking that fear somehow gives us a grip on things. We believe that by worrying and obsessing over every imaginable outcome, we can magically shield ourselves from the very thing we're most scared of—being left behind. But pause momentarily and think: What's the actual cost of all this worrying? Do these worries genuinely help your relationship or your well-being? Do they bring you closer in love and understanding, or do they sow the seeds of distance and separation?

The reality is that anxiety and fear, more often than not, don't do us any favors. They create a divide, keeping us from fully immersing ourselves in the love and happiness that exist right now, in this very moment. Even though it might sound counterintuitive, embracing an attitude of trust and letting go can pave the way to richer and more satisfying relationships. When you free yourself from the need to control everything, you open yourself to all the incredible opportunities that love and connection can offer.

Action Steps

In your journal, please write the name of your ego at the top of the page and draw what you think it looks like. Then, create talking bubbles over its head with the different things the ego likes to say to you. Take things a step further. Beneath this picture, write, "You are not me."

Breathing Through Anxiety: Practical Techniques

Self-awareness is a mighty and practical tool that can illuminate the path to understanding and managing the tricky attachment patterns we all wrestle with.[25] In the same way, a flashlight can highlight the way out of the dark; self-awareness serves as your lantern in the obscurity of anxious attachment patterns.

When you're self-aware, you can spot when those anxiety-driven thoughts are sneaking in and trying to call the shots. Instead of letting them control you, self-awareness gives you the power to transform those emotions into positive changes. Self-awareness is the skill that allows you to take a much-needed step back and watch your thoughts as if you're watching a movie. You're not the actor on the screen, but the one sitting in the theater, just watching.

And as you watch, you will see something unique unfold—your soul. Your soul is a wonderfully complex mosaic composed of numerous pieces that come together to form a beautiful picture of who you are. Within this collage, right at the center, you'll find your true self—that essence of you that's pure and overflowing with love.

This self of yours is the part that giggles with delight when you do something you love, feels a pang of empathy when you see someone struggling, and radiates a sense of calm when you take a deep breath and just be. And you know what? It's there, always available to you, ready to guide you through the twists and turns of life's journey.

Psychosynthesis can help you get to the center of yourself more often. Simply put, psychosynthesis is a holistic approach to understanding and nurturing all the different aspects of yourself. Psychosynthesis has also been described as a psychology of the self. Behind our many identifications resides a deeper knowledge of self that can be felt, nurtured, and strengthened with compassionate attention, a process Dr. Roberto Assagioli referred to as disidentification.[26] This approach believes you're not just a single identity but a collection of various parts, each with its own voice, desires, and wisdom. These parts might include your inner child, the responsible adult, the dreamer, and more.

This is only one technique for developing more extraordinary powers of self-awareness. Self-reflection exercises can also bring that sense of calm and presence. These exercises work like little adventures in your mind. For example, take a quiet moment to sit with your thoughts (maybe even write them down). Reflect on your reactions, your feelings, and your actions. Think about why you felt the way you did and what triggered the emotions.

Being mindful is a path that ultimately leads to increased self-awareness as well. Rowan, a vibrant 30-year-old librarian, found a sanctuary in mindfulness techniques. When waves of anxiety threaten, Rowan turns to the calming power of deep breathing and guided meditation. These routines serve as lifeboats to ride the waves of emotions rather than letting them take over. Embracing the here and now, instead of wrestling with the unknowns of tomorrow, tames the storm within.

A study published in the American Psychological Association on The positive effects of mindfulness on self-esteem adds scientific weight to the soothing effects of mindfulness.[27] Their research illuminates how "mindfulness significantly predicted increased self-esteem, which predicts overall life satisfaction."

Action Steps

Overcoming anxiety relies on gaining an objective perspective. The mindful practice of disidentification is a sure-fire exercise for giving you that detachment. It is a process of separating yourself from your thoughts, emotions, and ego to gain a more unbiased outlook on yourself. Here's a short daily exercise to help you practice disidentification:

- **Morning Reflection (5-10 minutes):** Begin your day with a few moments of stillness. Find a comfortable place to sit or lie down. Close your eyes, take a few deep breaths, and center yourself in the present moment. As thoughts, emotions, or self-identifications arise, observe them as if you're an impartial observer. Instead of saying, "I am anxious," simply acknowledge, "There is a feeling of anxiety." This subtle shift in language helps create distance between you and the experiences.

- **Throughout the day (1-2 minutes):** Set a timer

or use reminders on your phone to check in with yourself periodically. When the reminder goes off, pause whatever you're doing and take a few deep breaths. Notice your thoughts and emotions without judgment. Imagine them as passing clouds in the sky of your consciousness. Remember, you are the sky, not the clouds.

- **Evening Reflection (5–10 minutes):** Before bed, revisit your day. Reflect on moments when you successfully disassociated from your thoughts and emotions. Acknowledge the times when you got caught up in them, too. Without self-criticism, note these instances as opportunities for growth. As you drift off to sleep, remind yourself that your thoughts or emotions do not define you; you are the awareness that witnesses them.

This daily exercise gradually strengthens your ability to disidentify from your thoughts and emotions, helping you develop a more objective and peaceful relationship with your inner world.

Incorporating other mindful practices like this doesn't take much into your daily life. For example, this psychosynthesis exercise will take just a few minutes. Close your eyes and imagine a scene: a little child crying for help—that's your ego. Then, picture your higher self—the wiser, calmer you. Finally, see yourself as the observer, like a space that can move between these aspects. You're like a traveler, going from the crying child to the higher self and then to the observer. It's about being present from all of these perspectives.

Additionally, please take a few moments to immerse yourself fully in one activity, be it savoring a meal or feeling the sensation of water on your skin during a shower, cultivating mindfulness through sensory engagement. As worries arise, acknowledge them without getting entangled, envisioning them as leaves floating down a stream, allowing them to pass by rather than take hold. These practices are like keys that unlock a door to a calmer, more centered state of being, helping you reclaim control over anxiety's grip on your thoughts and emotions and, thus, your relationships.

Building a Toolbox: Developing Your Anxiety Management Plan

Overcoming anxiety is a profoundly personal journey where each person's path is as unique as their fingerprints. A personalized anxiety management plan guides you toward self-awareness and progress like a suit of armor.

Developing this toolkit starts with recognizing the triggers that often dance beneath the surface of your thoughts. Then comes practicing mindfulness to create a sanctuary of serenity in a sea of racing thoughts.

Another secret weapon against the grip of anxiety is cognitive-behavioral techniques. These strategies are tools for identifying and challenging negative thought patterns that feed the flames of tension. You can learn to unravel the threads of negative thoughts that once held you captive. Psychiatrists have shown how effective this is for anxiety and stress-related disorders.[28]

When navigating romantic relationships, incorporating cognitive-behavioral techniques can be your anchor against anxiety. One method is utilizing thought record sheets to analyze and reframe your anxious thoughts. Write down the situation, your thoughts, emotions, and evidence for and against those thoughts. Then, create a balanced perspective and more rational thoughts. Write those down, too!

Take things up a notch by including somatic exercises and nervine tonics to help regulate your nervous system and restore balance. Somatic exercises are conscious movements and focused attention done to release muscular tension and improve overall body awareness. This would be a great addition to your anxiety management plan if you suffer from chronic pain and movement limitations.

Nervine tonics are herbal remedies or substances that:

- Support and nourish the nervous system

- Promote relaxation
- Reduce stress
- Enhance overall nervous system function[29]

Common nervine herbs include chamomile, lavender, lemon balm, passionflower, and valerian.

Do you want to add something unconventional to your plan? How about shaking and vibrating after a traumatic experience to shake off the shackles of anxiety and reclaim your power? Grounding, breathing, and vibration are the three basic bioenergetic principles. "Bioenergetics" is a type of somatic therapy created by Alexander Lowen that "combines analysis of personality and character with body techniques and physical exercises to recognize and release chronic muscular tension."[30]

No anxiety management plan is complete without incorporating self-forgiveness. It's understanding that anxiety doesn't brand you as flawed, nor does it cast you as a burden on your relationships. Science reaffirms this and emphasizes how self-compassion is vital to taming anxiety's grip and boosting self-esteem.[31]

Also, nurture your self-assurance by embracing positive affirmations to counter those whispers of self-doubt that creep in when uncertainty clouds your mind. And don't be afraid to dip your toes into the waters of behavioral exposure; face those nerve-wracking conversations or vulnerability-sharing moments step-by-step, gradually desensitizing yourself to the fear that love's unpredictable terrain can bring. By threading these techniques into your everyday life, you're giving your mental compass a recalibration, equipping yourself to take on relationship-related anxiety with a more hopeful and proactive approach.

Meet Sophie. She is a 28-year-old whose anxiety management plan is a symphony of deep breathing exercises and heartfelt journaling. It's simple but effective, as she has woven her cocoon of tranquility into a haven where anxiety can't reach her as easily. And here's a scientific nod to the power of customization in 2020: the collective brain power of Thomeer and colleagues highlighted how having a personalized anxiety management plan can amplify the effectiveness of the techniques you choose to employ.[32]

By arming yourself with all these tools discussed above, you're not just facing anxious attachment patterns head-on; you're dismantling them piece by piece. With each step toward self-awareness, you're taking control of your reactions, building a healthier relationship foundation, and embracing the power to grow and transform.

Action Steps

Create a simple anxiety management plan with this step-by-step guide:

- **Self-Assessment:** Reflect on your anxiety triggers, symptoms, and how anxiety affects your daily life. Understand the situations, thoughts, and physical sensations contributing to your stress.

- **Set Clear Goals:** Define specific goals for managing your anxiety. These could be related to reducing the frequency of anxiety episodes, improving your ability to cope with triggers, or enhancing your overall well-being.

- **Choose Coping Strategies:** Select three coping strategies that resonate with you. These include relaxation techniques (deep breathing, progressive muscle relaxation), mindfulness practices, physical activities, creative outlets, and more. When you are comfortable with these, you can incorporate others.

- **Build a Routine:** Incorporate your chosen strategies into your daily routine. Allocate specific times for practicing relaxation exercises, engaging in mindfulness, or participating in activities that bring you joy.

Building the Foundation of Trust

∞

In relationships, trust is the bridge that connects two people. It's the feeling of safety and comfort when you know you can count on someone to be there for you. It's like having a friend who always keeps your secrets or a partner who supports your dreams. But trust in relationships isn't just one thing; it's a blend of emotions that make you feel secure, ideas that make you believe in the other person's intentions, and situations that prove their reliability. Like a recipe with different ingredients, trust in relationships requires a mix of these elements to make it solid and lasting.

And then there's self-trust, like a compass guiding you through life. It's that inner voice that says, "You've got this." You build self-trust by believing in your abilities and decisions. It's like knowing that even if things get tough, you'll find a way to navigate challenges. But, like trust in relationships, self-trust isn't a single, straightforward concept. It's an intricate combination of feelings of self-worth, belief in your capabilities, and situations where you've proven you can handle things.

This chapter invites you to explore trust—the fragile threads that connect us to others and the resilient bond that anchors us within ourselves. As we unravel the layers of trust's complexity, we will uncover a roadmap toward cultivating healthier connections and nurturing the garden of our self-worth.

The Role of Trust in Anxious Attachment

"I have trust issues."

It is unsettling how frequently we hear and perhaps say this statement. Trust issues are like having a protective shield around your heart and mind, making it hard to let people in. Once you've been hurt, you likely have this little voice in your head that constantly questions if you can trust someone new. This voice can be so loud that it is tough to believe in others, even when they've done nothing wrong.

Having trust issues is an increasingly common problem in today's world. Less than 20% of millennials confidently say they trust others, and that trust factor is only declining with every new generation.[33] It's not an issue that exists without reason. Our modern way of life has introduced several factors that can strain the trust between individuals in relationships.

One significant contributor to these issues is the digital age. With smartphones and social media, it's easier than ever for people to keep secrets or engage in activities that their partners may not know about. This digital deception can sow seeds of doubt and suspicion.

Communication, ironically, has become a double-edged sword. While we can communicate more quickly, the sheer volume of daily messages can lead to misunderstandings and mistrust. We've all experienced the confusion that can arise from a poorly worded text or an emoji misinterpretation.

Scrolling through social media, we often see curated versions of people's lives and relationships. The constant exposure to these seemingly perfect unions can make our relationships seem less genuine by comparison, raising questions about trust.

Our work lives can also take a toll. With demanding jobs and the ever-elusive work-life balance, we may have less time and emotional energy for our relationships, leading to doubts and insecurities about our partners' commitment.

Changing gender roles has brought new dynamics to relationships. While this is a positive step forward, some individuals may struggle with these shifts, leading to concerns about loyalty and intentions.

Psychological factors play a significant role, too. Rising stress, anxiety, and depression rates can make it harder to trust others due to heightened sensitivity and vulner ability.[34]

Past relationship traumas can cast long shadows. If someone has hurt you before, it's only natural to fear that it might happen again. Cultural and societal changes, evolving norms, and values surrounding relationships can also leave some people uncertain and mistrustful. Even our upbringing plays a role. Not having positive relationship role models during childhood can make it challenging to build trust in adulthood.[35]

Anxious attachment, characterized by a perpetual fear of abandonment, heightens the stakes of trust in relationships. The absence of faith can transform this fear into an all-consuming force that dictates thoughts, actions, and emotions. Simpson's pivotal study in 1990 showed trust can help us deal with all that fear and in security.[36]

Trust acts as a balm, soothing the wounds inflicted by past experiences and allowing for the possibility of genuine connection. Still, it isn't just about believing that your partner won't suddenly disappear. It's also about feeling confident they'll listen to your feelings and respect your boundaries. We sometimes forget to consider these things, especially when dealing with anxious attachment. We're so busy worrying about being left behind that we forget about how important it is that our emotions and limits are respected.

Trusting is not always easy. Anxious attachment messes with our heads, and sometimes we end up doubting ourselves. It's about telling that nagging voice of doubt to take a hike and giving yourself permission to be okay and enjoy the current moment without worrying about what "could be," "should be," or "would be." Learning to trust yourself is like finding a secret superpower within you; it allows you to bring your attention and awareness (your most valuable asset) to the present moment right here and now.

Journal Prompts

Use these journal prompts to strengthen your understanding of trust:

- Write about a time when trust was crucial in a relationship, either in relieving your fears or supporting your link with someone else. How did trust help you open up, discuss your emotions, and set healthy boundaries?

- What are some past instances where I trusted my instincts or decisions, and they turned out well? How can I use these positive experiences to build and strengthen my self-trust in current and future situations?

Cultivating Trust: From Self to Others to World

People tend to adopt three different mindsets regarding trust:

- Starting with trust until proven otherwise
- A neutral stance
- The need for trust to be earned due to skepticism

Despite the risks, the most effective approach is to start with trust, which means we must first make ourselves vulnerable. Vulnerability, often viewed as a weakness, emerges as a strength that paves the way for faith because you step into the unknown and find solid ground beneath. The truth is that trust begins with you. Instead of waiting for others to take the first step, embracing vulnerability initiates the journey toward a trust-rich environment, whether in life or in relationships.

If you're having trouble trusting yourself, trusting others will be tricky. But don't worry; self-trust is a skill you can build.

Here's how you pump up that self-trust muscle: Start by drawing lines in the sand and saying no when you mean no and yes when you mean yes because that's where it begins. Then there are your gut feelings. They're there for a reason. Honor them, even if they seem a bit quirky. And oh, the decisions you make— stand by them, even when unsure.

Let's talk about Amy. She's 26 years old, and trust is a bit of a tricky dance for her, especially the kind she needs for herself. She's got this habit of second-guessing everything, even what cereal to eat in the morning. Her brain is a busy bee that won't quit. But imagine if she could take a deep breath, make a choice, and stick with it. Her first step is trusting her judgments.

Do you know what else enables self-trust? Self-care and self-love. Take some time to show yourself the care and attention you deserve. Whether drawing, singing in the shower, or just sitting with your thoughts, those are like little love notes to yourself. Once you've got that self-trust thing going, trusting others becomes less like trying to find your way in the dark. You've got your very own flashlight now. When you know you have your own back, it's easier to believe that others won't bail on you.

How we perceive this journey called life defines our interaction with the world around us. Is It a mosaic of harsh realities or a canvas painted with love's hues? Our perspective isn't limited to life alone; it molds our perception of others and, equally important, of ourselves. To ride out life's ups and downs and keep an optimistic view of the world around us and ourselves in it, we need to put on the seatbelt of detachment.[37]

Detachment doesn't signify detachment from emotions or detachment from relationships. It represents something more nuanced – letting go of our yearning to control outcomes. It's a surrender to the currents of life, relinquishing the reins we often clutch so tightly. Giving up control is not a retreat from responsibility; it's an acknowledgment that life takes its course. It's an exercise in placing trust in the universe as it unfolds, even when its plan doesn't align with ours.

When you surrender, you're also embracing trust. Trusting that even though you can't control everything, life's got your back. It's that leap of faith that sets the stage for deeper connections. Think of it as opening the door to vulnerability. When you stop trying to control every little thing, love takes root and grows in unexpected ways. It's like watering a plant—you nurture it, and it flourishes.

Journal Prompts

Take out that sheet of paper again because we are going deep:

- Consider a recent circumstance where you started with trust, neutrality, or skepticism. How did this perspective affect your emotions and actions? How may embracing vulnerability have altered the outcome?

- Recall a decision you made that involved asserting your boundaries by saying yes or no with confidence. How did this reinforce your self-trust? Contrast this with a time when you questioned your choices. How could valuing your decisions, even amidst uncertainty, strengthen your self-trust?

- Explore the idea of detachment as surrendering the urge to control outcomes. Think of a situation where you felt a strong need for control. How might releasing this need and placing trust in the universe impact your experience? Reflect on times when life's unexpected course led to positive outcomes. How can you embrace this surrender and trust more often?

Building Trust in Relationships: A Step-by-Step Guide

A need for control can be closely related to anxious attachment. This need manifests as a strong desire or compulsion to have authority or dominance over situations, people, or events. Individuals with a strong need for control tend to engage in behaviors and actions aimed at micromanaging, manipulating, or regulating their surroundings to minimize perceived threats or uncertainties.

For instance, someone needing control in a relationship may constantly monitor their partner's actions, limit their independence, or insist on having the final say in all decisions. In a work setting, a person needing control might struggle with delegation, preferring to oversee every detail themselves. The need for control can manifest in different ways but often revolves around the belief that maintaining control is essential for personal safety, emotional stability, or achieving desired outcomes.

It's important to note that a need for control can have both positive and negative aspects. Sometimes, it can drive some people to be organized, responsible, and efficient. However, when taken to extremes, it can lead to issues in relationships, work, and overall well-being, as excessive control stifles creativity, hinders cooperation, and generates stress for both the individual and those around them.

Distinguishing between trust and control issues is tricky. When dealing with trust issues, there's often an overwhelming urge to maintain tight control over everything, driven by a fear of being hurt or deceived. For instance, imagine you're in a new romantic relationship, and your past experiences have left you wary. You might constantly check your partner's messages or question their every move, believing that this control will protect you from potential heartbreak. However, this controlling behavior can strain the relationship, making your partner feel suffocated and untrusted.

In reality, building trust requires a delicate balance. It's like learning to ride a bicycle. At first, you might be apprehensive, gripping the handlebars tightly to avoid falling. But as you gain confidence, you ease your grip to steer effectively. Trust is similar; you must loosen your control to allow room for honesty and vulnerability. So, instead of constantly checking your partner's messages, you gradually learn to trust their words and actions, allowing the relationship to grow.

While trust is the glue that keeps the pieces from falling apart in any relationship, it isn't built overnight; it's a journey, a step-by-step process that transforms mere connections into unbreakable bonds. Imagine it as a foundation you're laying for a house; every brick counts.

Let's break down this trust-building process into three pillars:

- **Open Communication:** Your feelings and thoughts are like puzzle pieces, like your partner's. When you share your pieces, fitting them together creates a complete picture. That's how open communication works. Being honest about your emotions and actively listening to your partner's feelings fosters trust and security.

- **Boundary Respect:** Setting boundaries is much like putting up personal space markers. Everyone has their comfort zones, which shows love and care when you respect them. Say your partner needs a breather after a rough day; honoring that space shows you trust their need for it. It sends a powerful message - "I respect you and your choices." Respect becomes the bridge that connects you both. We will be diving into this more in Chapter 5.
- **Consistency In Action:** Imagine trust as a delicate plant; consistency is the sunlight and water that helps it grow. Doing what you say, time and time again, builds a sense of reliability. If you promise to be there at a particular time, showing up speaks volumes. It's like crafting a track record of trustworthiness that makes your partner think, "Hey, I can count on this person."

When set right, these pillars create a structure that can weather the storms of doubt and uncertainty.

Remember, Building and nurturing trust is like tending a garden; it's an ongoing process that takes constant effort, understanding, and a hefty dose of patience. Sometimes, faith gets tested. Everyone makes mistakes. It's part of being human. What matters is how you deal with those hiccups. Imagine that your partner accidentally knocked over your favorite plant. What do you do? Open communication becomes your lifesaver. Talking things out, understanding each other's perspectives, and showing empathy can mend the relationship and even make it stronger.

Remember, trust-building isn't a one-time event; it's a process that unfolds step-by-step. Anxious attachment can make the process a little more laborious, but the beauty is that, with consistent effort, it's within your reach.

Journal Prompts

Here are a few journal questions to dive deeper into each of the three main ways to build trust:

- **Open Communication:** Think back to your recent talk with your partner. How did sharing your thoughts and feelings impact trust? Think about the benefits as well as the drawbacks of open conversation as a way to build a stronger relationship.
- **Boundary Respect:** Think about a time when you set a boundary. How did it affect trust and re-

spect? Consider how honoring boundaries contributes to a secure and trusting relationship.

- **Consistency in Action:** Think of a time when you followed through on a promise. How did this impact trust? Reflect on how reliability nurtures trust.

The Art of Drawing Lines

Setting Healthy Boundaries

∞

Imagine a warm summer afternoon at the park. You've agreed to meet a friend for a leisurely picnic. Your friend arrives with a big smile as you lay out the blanket and unpack the delicious spread you prepared. You both engage in meaningful conversations by sharing stories and laughter. As the sun begins to set, you notice that your energy is starting to wane. You kindly express that you need time to recharge and suggest meeting again soon. Your friend understands and thanks you for a beautiful day. You leave the park feeling content, knowing you respected your needs and communicated effectively.

Let's consider whether this scenario plays out differently. It's the same sunny day, and you're excited to spend time with your friend. Instead of acknowledging your need for space, your friend asks if you can stay longer because they're having a great time. They even add a pout and bat their eyes for good effect. Despite feeling drained, you agree to stay, suppressing your needs to avoid disappointing them. The sun sinks lower, and your energy plummets. You're physically exhausted and mentally drained, yet you continue to plaster on a smile. When you finally part ways, you leave feeling resentful and overwhelmed.

In the first scenario, maintaining healthy boundaries allowed you to enjoy the day while acknowledging your limits. You left feeling fulfilled and proud of your ability to care for yourself. In the second scenario, the anxious attachment tendencies led you to forsake your well-being to gain approval and validation.

The stark contrast between these scenarios highlights how crucial it is to recognize and address anxious attachment behaviors, including forsaking your boundaries. By setting healthy boundaries, you can foster genuine connections without sacrificing your mental and emotional well-being.

Don't lose hope if you recognize that you have not been good at maintaining boundaries. Setting and upholding boundaries is a learnable skill, like acquiring any other life skill, such as gaining proficiency in a new language, a musical instrument, or a sport. Like any other skill, it takes patience, consistent effort, and a willingness to adapt. With time and practice, you, too, can enhance your ability to create healthier, more balanced relationships through the effective method of boundary maintenance. Let reading this chapter be the first step in gaining this new skill.

Understanding the Importance of Healthy Boundaries

Boundaries act as a psychological fence between you and others, forming an essential tool in maintaining self-respect and preventing exploitation. Despite the image of division that the word 'boundary' can bring, it is not to be confused with emotional walls.[38] Emotional walls keep other people out and create emotional isolation, even if we are unaware we have erected them. On the other hand, boundaries are the subtle yet sturdy framework that shapes the contours of your relationships by enabling connection while preserving your sense of self.

Boundaries are similar to well-constructed fences in a garden that designate where one plot ends and another begins. Just as these fences don't obstruct the view of the plants or prevent their growth, healthy boundaries provide the space for relationships to flourish. Boundaries act as guides, signaling what is acceptable and what isn't, inviting open communication, and fostering trust. These boundaries create a protective space where your individuality thrives alongside your connections.

A clinical psychologist, Laura Markham, suggests that boundaries are pivotal in maintaining equilibrium and fending off resentment.[39] They provide a framework for balanced interactions, allowing us to give and receive without feeling overwhelmed or compromised. This equilibrium tips the scales toward healthier, more sustainable relationships.

Moreover, boundaries nurture feelings of safety and security, reducing anxiety associated with attachment dynamics. Take Li, a 37-year-old professional architect from China, as an example. By delineating boundaries around his work-life balance, he fortifies the edges of his relationships. This strategy permits him to maintain a thriving partnership in the company where he is a partner without the shadow of relentless work stress looming overhead.

There exists a spectrum of boundaries, each with its own distinct purpose and impact on the dynamics of relationships:

- **Physical Boundaries** are the outermost layer, governing your personal space and touch. They dictate who can come close and when setting the tone for comfort and intimacy.

- **Emotional Boundaries** delve deeper, guarding the sanctuary of your emotions and vulnerabilities. They determine how much you share, when, and with whom. Like a well-guarded treasure chest, emotional boundaries protect your innermost feelings from undue exposure.

- **Mental Boundaries** define your thoughts and opinions, drawing the line between open-mindedness and manipulation. These boundaries safeguard your intellectual autonomy, allowing you to engage in thoughtful discussions without feeling coerced.
- **Time Boundaries** mark the clock's territory, ensuring you allocate time for yourself, your pursuits, and your relationships. They prevent burnout by balancing your endeavors and your commitments.
- **Material Boundaries** encompass your possessions and resources. They guide your lending, borrowing, or sharing decisions, preserving your financial and material well-being.
- **Social Boundaries** extend to your interactions within various social circles. These boundaries help you navigate different relationships, maintaining distinct connections while avoiding excessive entanglement.
- **Digital Boundaries** is a modern addition, reflect-

ing your online presence and communication. They regulate your accessibility and exposure in the digital realm, protecting your privacy and mental space.

Understanding and implementing these diverse boundaries allows you to create a vibrant canvas of relationships that support your personal growth.

Journal Prompts

Setting boundaries will be difficult if you are uncertain of what they are. Here are a few journal questions to make those discoveries:

- What situations or interactions have left me feeling uncomfortable or drained recently?
- Are there any recurring patterns where I've felt my personal space invaded or my values compromised?
- What are the activities or relationships that energize me, and which ones leave me feeling depleted?"
- What behaviors or comments do I find unacceptable or disrespectful from others?

Techniques for Setting Healthy Boundaries

We deliberately gave you journal prompts that helped you understand your boundaries before we got to this section to make it more manageable. Identifying your boundaries is a crucial initial step in the process of enforcing them because it serves as the compass that guides your actions and interactions. Imagine embarking on a journey without a map or destination in mind; you'd likely end up lost or aimless. Similarly, without a clear understanding of your boundaries, you risk navigating your relationships and experiences without a sense of direction or purpose.

To establish boundaries, you must reflect on past experiences that elicited discomfort, feelings of being used, or lingering resentment. These emotional cues offer invaluable insights into areas where boundaries are required. For instance, consider Benjamin, a 45-year-old who recently became single. Benjamin dreamed of getting married and having a big family from when he was little. Therefore, when his marriage started falling apart, it was difficult for him to let go. In the process, he had his boundaries repeatedly infringed on. Through introspection, he recognized that the constant invasion of his privacy, like his partner checking his phone, was a source of discomfort. This realization allowed him to take that first step in establishing a vital boundary—identification. He follows up this step with the next—communicating this boundary.

Clear communication emerges as the linchpin when it comes to setting effective boundaries. The art lies in being assertive while maintaining respect and acknowledging that your needs are just as valid as the other person's.

It's also important to understand that boundaries are not rigid lines but dynamic expressions of self-care. As you evolve, your boundaries might need to change. Regular self-assessment ensures that these boundaries remain aligned with your evolving needs.

Action Steps

Building on the boundaries you identified from answering the journal questions earlier in this chapter, follow these steps:

- **Craft "I" Statements:** For each boundary you've identified, create "I" statements that clearly express your feelings and needs. For example, "I feel anxious and uneasy when personal topics are brought up during social gatherings because I value having a lighthearted atmosphere where I can enjoy the company of friends without delving into sensitive subjects."

- **Explain the Why:** Elaborate on the reasons behind each boundary. Write why maintaining this boundary is essential for your well-being and balance. For instance, "Maintaining a boundary around personal topics at social gatherings allows me to enjoy the setting without the pressure of explaining sensitive topics."

- **Clarify Consequences:** Clearly outline the potential consequences of crossing these boundaries. Mention how it might affect your emotional state, mental well-being, or the overall dynamics of the relationship. "If this boundary is crossed, it could increase stress and hinder my ability to relax and connect."

- **Practice Assertive Communication:** Enlist the help of a friend or family member, or even practice in front of a mirror. Practice delivering your "I" statements confidently and assertively, ensuring your message is clear and respectful.

Maintaining and Respecting Boundaries

Establishing boundaries brings an initial surge of empowerment, yet many of us face the challenge of steadfastly upholding them, notably when others are accustomed to your previous flexibility. It's essential to retain a firm grasp on your accepted limits while remaining flexible when circumstances warrant it. This principle extends to ensuring that others honor your boundaries and actively respect the boundaries of those around you.

Asserting yourself when your boundaries are compromised is fundamental to boundary maintenance. This act reinforces the importance of your borders and educates others about what is acceptable.

Just as we all have flavor preferences or preferred types of music, our limits are equally diverse and shaped by our life experiences, values, and personalities. Actions that appear utterly ordinary or innocuous to one person could inadvertently cross the boundary line of another. Picture this: Jane, an extroverted artist, thrives in lively social gatherings and cherishes spontaneity. She might consider popping by a friend's house unannounced as a delightful surprise. However, her friend Michael, a more introverted and structured individual, values his personal space and routine. To him, an uninvited visit might feel like an invasion of his solitude.

Navigating these differences requires a nuanced understanding that we all have different comfort zones. Cultivate empathy and respect for these variations, and your relationships will thrive. Discovering that you've inadvertently crossed someone else's boundaries can be a moment of reflection and growth. Handling this situation with sensitivity and accountability is essential to maintaining healthy relationships. Here's a step-by-step guide on what to do if you find out you've crossed someone else's boundaries:

- **Recognize and Reflect:** First, acknowledge the situation. If someone expresses discomfort or you notice signs of distress, take a moment to reflect on your actions and their potential impact.

- **Pause and Apologize:** If you realize you've crossed a boundary, don't hesitate to apologize sincerely. Taking responsibility for your actions demonstrates respect for the other person's feelings.

- **Listen Attentively:** Give them space to express their feelings, whether it's frustration, discomfort, or disappointment. Active listening shows that you value their perspective and are committed to understanding their point of view.

- **Seek Clarification:** Ask for more information about what specific boundary you crossed, which is also an excellent time to ask about any other regulations that this person would like you to honor. It demonstrates your willingness to learn and adjust your behavior in the future.

- **Avoid Defensiveness:** It's natural to feel defensive but resist that urge. Instead, focus on empathy and understanding their emotions.

- **Learn and Adapt:** Use this experience as an opportunity for growth. Reflect on how you can be more mindful of boundaries in the future, both with this person and in general.

- **Respect Their Response:** Accept that the other person may need time to process and decide how to proceed. Give them space, and respect their feelings and decisions.

- **Make Amends:** Depending on the situation, consider whether there's a way to make amends involving changing your behavior or offering support.

- **Stay Mindful:** From now on, be more conscious of boundaries in your interactions. Ask for consent when needed, and pay attention to verbal and non-verbal cues.

- **Rebuild Trust:** It might take time to rebuild trust, especially if the boundary violation is significant. Consistently respecting their boundaries in the future will contribute to rebuilding trust over time.

Remember, we're all humans, and we all make mistakes. The key is handling those mistakes and using them as opportunities for personal growth and improved relationships. Just as learning to ride a bike involves a few falls before getting the hang of it, navigating boundaries requires learning from missteps to foster stronger connections. Just be mindful to maintain your limits while respecting other people's.

Action Steps

Take a moment for introspection and growth by reflecting on the evolution of your boundaries. Consider the changes in your circumstances and personal development since you initially set your boundaries. Ask yourself if your current boundaries still align with your needs and values. Are they effectively supporting your well-being and relationships? Engage in this self-assessment regularly, allowing yourself the flexibility to adjust and adapt your boundaries as you grow.

∞

Your Review Can Help Others

> "To serve one is to serve all." - The Law of One, Carla Rueckert

Are you ready to be a catalyst for change in the world of relationships? As you continue your journey through this book, you're not just embarking on a personal exploration - you're stepping into a role that can transform the lives of countless others.

Help us share this knowledge and experience with others so they can have more of what we all genuinely desire—love.

If you've found value in the pages you've read thus far, we encourage you to share your insights with those who could benefit.

Every word you write in your review is a step towards a revolution in relationships. By sharing your experiences and the wisdom you've gained, you're helping others chart their course toward the love and intimacy they desire.

Simply by expressing how this book has enriched your life and what lies within its pages, you'll help others grasp that love isn't just an emotion; it's a dynamic force that requires action and unwavering commitment.

Thank you for joining us in our mission to serve others through the power of love and understanding. Together, we illuminate the path to deeper connections and lasting joy.

Trigger Happy

Identifying and Managing Anxiety Sparks

∞

There's an ancient Cherokee Indian legend that encapsulates one of the most pivotal battles waged within us.[40] The tale starts with an elder Cherokee imparting wisdom to his eager grandson about life. "Son," he says. "A fight is going on inside me."

The elder elaborates, "It's a terrible fight, and it is between two wolves. One is evil; he is anger, envy, sorrow, regret, greed, arrogance, self-pity, guilt, resentment, inferiority, lies, false pride, superiority, and ego."

He pauses for good effect because no story is complete without some tension, then continues, "The other is good—he is joy, peace, love, hope, serenity, humility, kindness, benevolence, empathy, generosity, truth, compassion, and faith. The same fight is happening inside you and every other person, too."

The young man contemplates this before asking, "Which wolf will win?"

With the wisdom of ages, the old Cherokee answers simply, "The one you feed."

We inadvertently grant them fertile ground to flourish by perpetually nurturing anxiety and fear. We need to learn to withhold sustenance from the anxious wolf. Doing so means recognizing it the moment it bares its teeth. Achieving this insight demands recognizing the tools at play. The ego-driven wolf wields tools of anxiety, fear, guilt, shame, blame, and judgment. Whenever we find ourselves entangled in fight, flight, fawn, or freeze responses, it's a telltale sign that the ego wolf is at the helm. Its methods are executed through a repertoire of defense mechanisms, steering our actions and reactions.

Gaining a foothold in this fight begins with acknowledging that you are distinct from the triggers that seem to wield control. The ever-vigilant ego orchestrates these triggers, which operate in the subconscious. Though often seen as a source of frustration, this aspect of ourselves is rooted in fear—the fear of wounds yet to heal. It's vital to navigate this terrain with a gentle approach, one where there is no blame or judgment. Instead, envision it as your inner child just wanting to be loved.

Believing in the potency of these triggers unwittingly nourishes the "bad" wolf within you. The more attention you lavish on it, the more robust it becomes. You inevitably diminish its influence on you by diverting your focus from this wolf of fear and anxiety; this leaves room to nourish the benevolent wolf in you. This chapter is designed to help you feed the "good" wolf.

The Landmines Within: Recognizing Your Triggers

Triggers are powerful emotional catalysts that activate intense reactions within us based on past experiences and deeply ingrained fears.[41] These triggers can manifest as specific situations, words, or actions that evoke strong emotional responses, often disproportionate to the current context. For example, a person who has experienced betrayal might feel a surge of anger and mistrust when their partner is late without explanation, even if the lateness is unrelated to betrayal. Similarly, someone who has faced rejection in the past might find themselves overwhelmed by anxiety and self-doubt when faced with a situation where their contribution is critiqued. Triggers can evoke a range of emotions, such as fear, sadness, anger, or even joy, and they offer valuable insights into the complex interplay between our past, present, and emotional well-being.

People with anxious attachments display many defensive mechanisms that act as coping strategies when faced with perceived threats to their emotional connections and relationships. These mechanisms, often automatic and subconscious, are triggered by deep-seated fears of abandonment or rejection rooted in past experiences. Anxious attachment defense mechanisms are meant to minimize the discomfort of these fears and maintain a sense of connection, even if they may not always be helpful or healthy in the long run.

Examining these defense mechanisms offers a wealth of insights into our emotional triggers. Each mechanism is like a clue, inviting us to look at why we react the way we do and uncover the connections between our past stories and today's emotions. These triggers can look like:

- **Engaging in Persistent Infidelity Checks:** This entails persistently snooping, cross-checking, and closely examining our partner's behaviors, such as their phone usage or online interactions, all in the quest to uncover signs of potential betrayal. This conduct gradually erodes trust in the relationship and nurtures insecurity that paradoxically feeds the fears we're trying to alleviate.

- **Undermining Others:** This involves lowering others' worth through comparisons, belittling comments, or unfavorable comparisons in a misguided effort to elevate our self-esteem.[42] Regrettably, this approach only fuels a cycle of negativity, pushing us farther away from the very love and connection we yearn for.

- **People-pleasing:** Also referred to as martyrdom, this contact self-sacrifice means we neglect our needs, stifle our opinions, and place other people's needs ahead of our own. Despite its facade of selflessness, this approach eventually breeds resentment and self-neglect and sets the stage for an imbalanced power dynamic within relationships.

- **Undermining Your Self-Worth:** This stems from embracing the belief that our existence hinges entirely on the relationships in our lives or relying solely on a particular person, like our partner, for a sense of identity and self-value. This perspective erases our individuality and erodes our self-esteem, leaving us susceptible to waves of anxiety and haunting worries about abandonment.

- **Infidelity:** Pursuing validation and a false sense of security through extramarital affairs or keeping backup relationships in case of potential solitude can also serve as a defense mechanism for anxious attachment. Unfortunately, this erodes trust and fuels a cycle of emotional detachment and distance.

- **Believing You Can Read Minds:** This translates into falling into the trap of assuming we can decipher the thoughts and emotions of others without engaging in open communication. Often, this phantom ability leads to leaping to pessimistic conclusions. This penchant for mind-reading nurtures feelings of insecurity, fuels misunderstandings, and needlessly stokes conflicts.

- **Crystal Ball Gazing:** This act of fortune-telling paints dire scenarios onto the canvas of the future, convincing us that the worst possible outcomes are destined to unfold. This art of predicting doom feeds the hungry monster of anxiety, barricading us from fully embracing the present with a sense of trust and openness.

- **Simplistic Tagging:** This sign involves sticking rigid labels onto ourselves, our partners, and the connections we share. Examples include "He's an idiot" or "I will never be enough." This stark, black-and-white mindset shackles our capacity to appreciate the complex shades of growth and potential that exist within us and those around us.

- **Overgeneralizing:** Painting with broad strokes

can be deadly to our relationships. Dipping our verbal brush in absolutes like "always" or "never" to describe events or behaviors brushes aside delicate subtleties and leaves room for evolution. This cognitive twist reinforces negative beliefs, blinding us to the glimmers of positivity within our relationships.

- **Catastrophizing:** The "bad" wolf can give us the outline that everyday hurdles are insurmountable challenges. This gives us the sense that we're powerless without other people or that minor setbacks will be our downfall. This catastrophic thinking feeds anxiety while choking off our res ilience.[43]

- **Playing the Victim:** This involves treating every situation as our spotlight, convinced that every move and moment reflects our worth. This ego-driven performance nurtures guilt and shame and heightens the fear of being left alone in the limelight.

- **Being Controlling:** We embody this when we try to choreograph every step another person takes, whether that person is our partner, friend, colleague, child, or other. This tight grip chokes trust and smothers the possibility of authentic connections.

- **Nagging:** This is a persistent tune of criticism, constant reminders, and meticulous oversight to maintain control of the relationship and gain reassurance. This behavior only leads to frustration, resentment, and a chilling absence of emotional intimacy.

- **Seeking Constant Reassurance:** This relies heavily on our partners' external applause and ceaseless affirmations to soothe our worries and doubts. While a sprinkle of encouragement is nourishing, an excess of it becomes like a sugary treat—delicious yet eventually cloying and emotionally draining for both sides.

- **Conflict Avoidance:** Conflict is a natural part of life. While we should not actively try to fan the flames of it, shying away from disagreements or skirmishes out of fear of abandonment or rejection is equally toxic. The evasion prevents growth, hinders effective communication, and perpetuates a stagnant relationship dynamic.

These behavioral patterns, seemingly a shield against uncertainty, are, in truth, a self-fulfilling prophecy. Like a tangled web, they trap us in cycles of fear and insecurity, reinforcing the same concerns they aim to reduce. Each act of nagging, each plea for constant reassurance, each sidestep of conflict, casts a vote of no-confidence in the relationship, building walls that distance us from the very connection we desire.

Journal Prompts

Think about behaviors in your life that might be causing issues in your relationships—things like overreacting, being overly defensive, or constantly seeking validation. For the next week, watch for moments when you catch yourself doing these things. Write down what triggered this behavior, your emotions, and what happened.

This activity is all about raising your self-awareness and setting the stage for positive changes:

- Take a behavior, like getting overly defensive, for example. How does this behavior make your fears and insecurities worse instead of better? Think about how it creates a cycle that erodes trust and intimacy. Then, consider what you can do to break this cycle and replace it with healthier responses. Imagine how making these changes might lead to more genuine and fulfilling connections.

- Now, pick a defense mechanism you often rely on;

maybe it's always trying to please others. Reflect on times when you've fallen into this pattern. What were the situations that triggered it, and what emotions were driving your actions? Think about how it impacted your relationships with others and your sense of self. This reflection can help you see how addressing these mechanisms could lead to better ways of handling challenging situations.

- Next, come up with a positive alternative response to that defense mechanism you identified. Imagine how adopting this new response could make a positive difference in your life and your relationships. Pay attention to when the old behavior starts to crop up as you go about your day. Challenge yourself to choose this new, healthier response you've thought of.

Keep a journal to track your progress, and note how these changes in your behavior influence your interactions and overall emotional well-being over time. This way, you'll see the real impact of your efforts to improve your relationships.

The Firefighter Within: Strategies for Managing Your Ego's Triggers

Spotting triggers is only the beginning. The real magic happens when you tackle those spooks head-on, and that's where trigger management steps in. Leah had this lightbulb moment when talking about her partner chatting with other women. The discussion hit her panic button labeled "Abandonment Fear!" She grabbed her courage and spoke with her partner about her feelings. Her partner responded, "Oh, that's why you've been giving me the side-eye!" Understanding blossomed, trust grew as he reassured her of the platonic nature of the interactions, and her fear shrank.

Carlos had a similar "a-ha" moment. Hearing about his band of friends going on an outing without him had him feeling left out. But instead of letting those vibes crash his party, he took charge. He took himself out on a solo date night, and his confidence got a workout. He found that he didn't need others to validate him to have a great time.

Empower yourself in the same way by using the Anxious Attachment Recovery Technique:

Step 1: Recognize the Source of Thought

Establish a mindful distance between yourself and your thoughts by remembering a fundamental truth—this is not *you* having this thought. During episodes of anxiety, the intensity can be overwhelming, consuming your attention. However, this is the time you need to step up to the plate and grasp the distinction between you and your thoughts. Your thoughts are not your essence; they're merely mental occurrences.

Pause, take a deep breath, and acknowledge that anxious thoughts don't define your identity. Whenever fear or anxiety emerges, practice recognizing that these thoughts aren't originating from your core self. Instead, they're responses from the ego.

Step 2: Break the Cycle and Reclaim Your Power

You must remove their hold over you to effectively manage anxiety and fear. Take back your power. Recognize that anxiety and fear reside within your thoughts, not in the present moment. Inhale deeply and center your awareness on the here and now. Engage with the ground beneath your feet, observe the sensations coursing through your body, and reconnect with your senses.

The present holds a treasure trove of beauty and the potential to free you from the clutches of anxiety.

Breaking the toxic pattern isn't always that easy, so sometimes you need to infuse a bit of humor into the situation. Laugh, tell a joke, or even do a dance—whatever it takes to shake off those anxious thoughts. It might seem silly, but that is the point. These moments of playfulness are medicine for the soul. They remind you that life is for enjoyment, that your identity surpasses your concerns, and that you have the strength to rise above any challenge. So, embrace the light moments and let our spirit ascend the plain of worry and tension through laughter and movement.

Here are a few more suggestions for getting out of an anxious state:

- Counteract the urge to slouch or withdraw by curling into a ball by adopting the "Superman" pose.[44] Place your hands on your hips, lift your chin, expand your chest, and reaffirm your inherent strength.

- When you notice a frown forming, deliberately and gradually curve the corners of your lips into a broad smile. Do this until your body responds and shifts its demeanor.

- If you sense trembling, unease, or a lack of efficacy in other ways, consider the physiological effect of deliberate shaking and vibrating. This action can help recalibrate your nervous system, signaling that the "fight or flight" response has elapsed and the present moment has returned.

- Breathe intentionally because it has been scientifically proven that deliberate and unhurried breathing has a calming influence on your nervous system.[45]

Step 3: Practice the Catalyst Journal Technique to Uncover Negative Thoughts and Attached Emotions

The Law of One philosophy is a spiritual concept that emphasizes the interconnectedness of all existence.[46] This philosophy suggests that every individual and experience in our lives is interconnected and catalyzes our personal growth and spiritual evolution. The Catalyst Journal Technique is a practical tool derived from this philosophy, allowing us to uncover negative thoughts and their emotions. By engaging in this practice, we can better understand ourselves and work towards transforming these negative patterns into positive ones.

Embrace this philosophy with this journal exercise:

- **Reflect on a catalyst** (a challenging experience, particularly one that triggered feelings of sadness, anger, or fear).

- **Identify the emotions** that surged during this catalyst. (All negative emotions distill into sadness, anger, or fear.) Arrange these emotions in the order you felt them.

- **Pinpoint the belief** connected to the specific emotion experienced. (Sadness often links to a sense of lack, anger to attachment, and fear to a desire for control.)

- **Ask yourself these two questions:** What does this experience prompt me to accept and forgive within myself? What does this experience encourage me to become more aware of within myself?

This self-reflection allows us to acknowledge and forgive ourselves for past mistakes or shortcomings contributing to these negative thoughts and emotions. It also identifies and addresses negative thoughts and the feelings they invoke, ultimately fostering self-awareness and growth.

Step 4: Challenge and Transform Negative Thoughts

Clenched in the grip of fear, reality can seem terrifying, but this is just a veil cast over your eyes by the ego. Stop fear from blinding you by stretching its limits and scrutinizing its validity through cognitive restructuring.

Cognitive restructuring is a technique to recognize and challenge negative thoughts and replace them with more realistic and positive ones. Practice the following exercise to help reshape your outlook and foster adaptive and secure beliefs. Close your eyes and take a deep breath. Think about the views that may have become deeply rooted within you—thoughts like "I am unworthy of love" or "I am destined to be abandoned." While these beliefs might have crystallized due to past experiences, they do not dictate your present or future.

Acknowledge their existence, but do not give them control over you. Ask yourself: "Is there concrete evidence to support this thought?" or "Could there be another way to interpret this situation?" By questioning your negative thoughts, you can free yourself from their clutches by reframing them into more realistic and affirmative perspectives.

You can apply cognitive reframing to your life at any time. Let's say you're in a new relationship, and your partner takes longer than usual to respond to your message. Rather than assuming the worst, engage in this exercise:

- **Identify the negative thought:** "They neglect me because they're indifferent."

- **Challenge the thought:** Is there any concrete proof to support this belief? Is there an alternative explanation?

- **Reframe with substantiated evidence and alternative perspectives:** Recall occasions when they showed affection and consideration. Ponder the likelihood that they might be occupied or preoccupied rather than deliberately neglecting you.

Remember, your identity isn't tethered to your past or to the beliefs you once held. You can rewrite your narrative, shaping a story of love and high self-worth.

Step 5: Embrace the Self: Self-Compassion, Self-Care, Self-Love, and Self-Celebration

Nourish the tactics that feed your inner "good" wolf; even wolves enjoy a hearty meal. The ingredients for that meal can include:

- **Practice Mindfulness:** Engage in mindfulness exercises to stay present, foster self-awareness, and reduce the grip of anxious thoughts.

- **Practice Positive Self-Talk:** Counter negative self-talk with positive affirmations that remind you of your strengths and worth.
- **Physical Activity:** Engage in regular physical activity, whether it's a walk, yoga, or exercise, to release endorphins and alleviate anxiety.
- **Opt for Healthy Lifestyle Practices:** Prioritize proper sleep, nutrition, and hydration to provide your body and mind with the necessary support.
- **Use Creative Outlets:** Express yourself through creative endeavors like art, writing, or music, which can serve as therapeutic outlets for your emotions.
- **Social Connection:** Maintain connections with friends and loved ones who provide support and understanding during anxious times.
- **Reward Yourself:** Acknowledge your accomplishments, no matter how small, and treat yourself to something enjoyable as a form of self-celebration.
- **Mindful Activities:** Engage in activities that bring you joy and engage your senses, like reading, gardening, or cooking, to create moments of

mindfulness and self-appreciation.

Please give yourself a standing ovation for navigating to the other side of your triggers and transforming them into a stepping stone for your evolution. Imagine it like a graduation ceremony but for mastering life's challenges.

Key Takeaways

Identifying triggers that cause anxious thoughts is a great start to overcoming them. The real magic happens when you confront those triggers head-on. To manage anxiety, practice recognizing that your thoughts aren't your core identity, challenge negative thoughts, and embrace self-care techniques that strengthen your inner positivity.

Boosting Your Worth

Techniques for Building Self-Esteem

∞

Self-esteem is all about how we see and feel about ourselves. It's like having a personal mirror that reflects how we view our worth, abilities, and uniqueness. Solid self-esteem means embracing our true selves, flaws and all, and recognizing our incredible strengths and qualities. When we have high self-esteem, we feel confident and believe in our value, whether in our relationships, accomplishments or simply being our authentic selves.

Unfortunately, the statistics surrounding low self-esteem paint a concerning picture, particularly for women. Research reveals that a significant portion of women, approximately 80%, experience moments of self-doubt and struggle with low self-esteem at some point in their live s.[47] Factors such as societal pressures, unrealistic beauty standards, and gender inequality contribute to this disparity. Moreover, studies indicate that women are more likely than men to internalize criticism and negative feedback,[48] amplifying the impact on their self-esteem.

Men are not exempt from similar feelings of inadequacy, though. According to a 2021 Gee Hair survey conducted by *Censuswide,*[49] a significant number of men struggle with low self-esteem. Approximately 55% of men in the study expressed that they do not believe others like them. Additionally, the survey revealed that about 4 out of 5 men do not see themselves as attractive, and a staggering 60% lack confidence in their job performance. Furthermore, nearly half of the men surveyed indicated they do not perceive themselves as intelligent.

We have established that low self-esteem is an epidemic, but what is this sickness exactly? Low self-esteem is a persistent feeling of inadequacy, worthlessness, and self-doubt. Think of it as wearing tinted glasses that distort your perception of yourself. Those lenses cause you to focus on only the things you see as your flaws and shortcomings, overlooking your strengths and positive qualities.

It's tough when you're constantly battling low self-esteem. Malaya, a store manager from a Filipino family, knows these feelings all too well. Her days are a struggle—a constant fight against the negative thoughts that invade her mind and color her perception of herself. She wakes up in the morning, and even before her feet hit the ground, a little voice inside her head starts whispering,

"You're not good enough. You're a failure." The broken record plays on repeat, chipping away at her confidence and leaving her feeling defeated before the day even begins.

Simple tasks become mountains to climb. Making a phone call, sending an email, or even just stepping outside the comfort of her home feels like an impossible challenge. There is a lot of pressure on her as the eldest first-generation member of her immigrant family, and she is convinced that people are judging her, scrutinizing her every move, and finding her wanting. So she withdraws, hiding away in the safety of solitude, where the judgment of others feels a little less suffocating.

Social situations are no easier for this young lady. It's like walking on eggshells. She chooses every word she speaks very carefully, every action meticulously calculated, all in a desperate attempt to avoid making a fool of herself. Office get-togethers are the worst, according to her estimations! She becomes hyperaware of every perceived flaw, from how she looks to how she speaks. It's exhausting—she's constantly second-guessing herself and wondering if she'll ever measure up.

Perhaps the most heartbreaking part is how low self-esteem seeps into every corner of her life, tainting even the moments of joy. She has achieved many great things—things no one else in her family has—and instead of celebrating, the voice in her head whispers, "It was just luck. You don't deserve this." The idea that she does not deserve happiness or success makes her accomplishments seem hollow.

It's a lonely battle, too. On the outside, she appears confident and put together by everyone she meets and those who know her, but inside, she's crumbling. She yearns for someone to see through the facade and understand her pain, but the fear of judgment keeps her silent. So, she suffers in silence, feeling isolated and misunderstood.

Can you relate to what Malaya feels? The numbers say that the probability is high that you indeed do. Millions of people across all genders and continents fight similar inner demons. While it may feel overwhelming, there is hope. You deserve love and acceptance from others and, most importantly, yourself.

Your day-to-day life might resemble Malaya's to a tee, but we invite you to imagine a world where your self-esteem shines bright, you radiate confidence from within, and you no longer seek validation from others to feel worthy. It's a world where self-love and acceptance are your guiding lights, empowering you to embrace your true worth and live a fulfilling life. We wrote this chapter to help you cross the bridge and get to that place.

Unmasking the Self-Esteem Anxious Attachment Link

Why did low self-esteem and anxious attachment become partners in relationships? Because they heard it was a "clingy" job opportunity and thought, "Hey, we're perfect for this!" Talk about insecurities sticking together!

We don't blame you if you rolled your eyes and questioned our sanity with that joke, but while we try to make light of the serious matter of anxious attachment, it is no laughing matter. Low self-esteem and anxious attachment often form a tangled dance within relationships where our insecurities can make us feel unsure about our connections. When we don't feel good enough, we might seek constant validation from others, becoming clingy and terrified of being left behind.

In the vibrant city of Buenos Aires, there lived a remarkable woman named Nelida. At 28 years old, she exuded an infectious zest for life. She possessed various talents and had achieved many significant milestones in her personal and professional lives. However, beneath her radiant exterior, Nelida grappled with a deep-seated fear of rejection and abandonment that stemmed from her attraction to members of the same sex.

Nelida had always known that her true self differed from societal expectations. She had discovered her authentic identity as a lesbian, which brought her immense joy and fulfillment. However, the fear of being rejected by her family loomed over her like a dark cloud. This fear of rejection was a constant companion, leading to low self-esteem.

In her pursuit of love and acceptance, Nelida often sought validation from her partner. She yearned for external reassurance to counteract the internal doubts that plagued her. Her fear of abandonment caused her to hold on tightly, afraid that she would lose the love and connection she so desperately craved if she let go.

Unfortunately, this need for validation placed a significant strain on their relationship. Nelida's partner, understanding the depth of her insecurities, tried their best to provide support and reassurance. However, the weight of Nelida's constant need for validation became overwhelming, creating a cycle that threatened the foundation of their love.

Nelida's story highlights that the quest for self-acceptance and validation does not confine itself to a specific demographic. It transcends all walks of life and affects individuals from unique backgrounds.

Amid the challenges, Nelida's journey also shows the resilience and strength that can emerge from the depths of self-doubt. She and her partner eventually broke up, yet Nelida rose like a phoenix from the ashes of the darkest moment of her life.

She bravely confronted her fears and shared her most authentic self with her family. Did some accept her as she was? Yes. Also, some didn't. But the most important thing the experience taught Nelida was that her worth did not depend on the approval of others. She learned that proper validation comes from within, from embracing her unique identity and finding the courage to love herself unconditionally.

We can all learn something from her journey: relying on external tactics to feel approved always makes us feel like we've fallen short. We must shift our focus inward and find validation within ourselves.

Building healthy self-esteem starts with recognizing our strengths, embracing our imperfections, and understanding that we're worthy. We must challenge those negative thoughts that hold us back and replace them with kinder, more empowering ones. It's like flipping the script and giving ourselves a pep talk.

Another piece of the puzzle is self-acceptance. We've got to let go of trying to fit into society's molds and seeking validation from others. Embracing our quirks and unique qualities is what makes us extraordinary. When we do that, we can build genuine connections based on authenticity and respect—no more faking it or bending backward to please.

Here's the secret sauce: developing an internal sense of control. By that, we mean trusting our judgment and finding happiness from within. We don't need others to tell us we're doing okay. We've got this. Letting go of clingy behaviors and the fear of being left behind becomes more manageable when we rely on ourselves for fulfillment.

Keeping it real, we know that this isn't an overnight transformation. It takes time and effort. We're talking baby steps, self-compassion, and a commitment to personal growth.

Journal Prompts

This journal exercise aims to help you recognize the interplay between low self-esteem, anxious attachment, and the impact of seeking external affirmation. By exploring these dynamics, you can gain insights into your patterns and work toward fostering a healthier sense of self-worth and secure attachments.

As usual, set aside dedicated time in a quiet, comfortable space to reflect and write freely. Begin by exploring your self-esteem:

- Reflect on moments when you have felt unsure about your worth or experienced self-doubt. Write down specific instances or patterns that come to mind.

- Consider the possible sources of these feelings.

Were they influenced by societal expectations, past experiences, or relationships?

- Write about how low self-esteem has affected your thoughts, emotions, and behaviors, particularly when seeking external affirmation.

Shift your focus to anxious attachment:

- Reflect on your past or current relationships. Have you noticed any clingy behaviors or fears of abandonment? Write about specific instances that come to mind.

- Explore the underlying emotions driving these behaviors. Are they rooted in a fear of rejection, a need for validation, or a lack of self-assurance?

Recognize the impact of seeking external affirmation:

- Explore how seeking validation from others has influenced your self-esteem and attachment patterns. Have you relied on external sources for your sense of worth?

- Reflect on the consequences of depending solely on external affirmation. Have you experienced feelings of clinginess or fear of desertion when that validation is not readily available?

Building Self-Esteem: The Foundation of Secure Attachment

Let's flip the switch for Malaya. In this scenario, she values herself and her contribution to her workplace, family, friends, and more. She wakes up in the morning and looks in the mirror with a genuine smile, knowing she embraces her true self and loves every aspect of her being. Just as we flipped the switch for Malaya, you, too, can elevate the vibrations you send out into the universe, attracting a life that brings out the pure energy in you.

You might not understand what that looks like, so let's paint the picture. Valuing yourself means setting boundaries that protect your time, energy, and well-being and feeling empowered to say no to things that don't align with your values or bring you joy. It's surrounding yourself with people who uplift and support you and letting go of toxic relationships that drain your spirit. Valuing yourself can be celebrating your accomplishments, big or small, and recognizing your unique talents and abilities. It's allowing yourself to indulge in self-care activities that nourish your body, mind, and soul. It's speaking kindly to yourself and offering encouragement and forgiveness when you make mistakes.

Pursue your passions and embrace new opportunities with a sense of self-assurance. It's standing up for your beliefs, even if it means going against the crowd. It's embracing imperfections and understanding that they are part of what makes you beautifully human. Valuing yourself is finding joy in the simple moments, appreciating the beauty around you, and being grateful for the gift of life. It's living authentically, with a deep sense of self-acceptance, knowing that you deserve love, happiness, and all the incredible experiences life has to offer.

This picture does not have to remain in your mind. It can become a reality. One technique that can work wonders for boosting your self-esteem is using positive affirmations.

Imagine you're at a bustling farmer's market, browsing through colorful stalls filled with fruits and vegetables. As you approach the juicy, ripe apples, your eyes light up excitedly. You pick one up, feeling its weight and admiring its vibrant color. Think of your thoughts and emotions as magnets, like the apple in your hand. The law of attraction suggests that the energy you emit through your thoughts and feelings attracts similar energy back to you,[50] just like a magnet attracts objects. If you radiate positivity, gratitude, and belief in your dreams, you're like a magnet for positive experiences and opportunities.

Conversely, dwelling on negativity, doubt, and fear might attract more of those experiences. So, just like choosing the juiciest apple at the farmer's market, you can choose the thoughts and emotions you want to cultivate. By consciously focusing on positivity, visualizing your goals, and taking aligned action, you can magnetize the desired things, drawing them closer to you in a beautiful dance of attraction.

Positive affirmations allow you to direct your energy and thoughts intentionally. So, instead of letting negative thoughts like "I am not worthy of love" take over, remind yourself with conviction that "I am deserving of unconditional love."

Let's look at how positive affirmations can transform a person's life. Meet Mel, a vibrant 35-year-old woman from South Africa. For years, Mel struggled with self-confidence and battled persistent self-doubt. She often questioned her abilities, feared rejection, and felt unworthy of love and success.

While searching for ways to improve her self-esteem, Mel stumbled upon the concept of positive affirmations. Intrigued, she gave it a try. Every morning, she stood in front of the mirror, looked herself in the eyes, and repeated powerful statements like, "I am capable and deserving of success," "I am enough just as I am," and "I am worthy of love and respect."

At first, it felt awkward and silly. Mel's inner critic whispered doubts in her ear, but she persisted, recognizing that change often begins outside our comfort zones. With each repetition, Mel felt a glimmer of hope, a spark of belief that maybe, just maybe, she could rewrite the negative script that plagued her for so long.

As the days turned into weeks, Mel noticed subtle shifts within herself. Instead of automatically dismissing compliments, she learned to accept them with gratitude and began to trust her abilities, taking on new challenges and celebrating her achievements. The affirmations became her daily reminder that she was capable, worthy, and deserving of all life's good things, which wasn't just a surface-level change. Neuroplasticity, the brain's ability to rewire and form new neural connections,[51] played a significant role in Mel's transformation. With each repetition of the positive affirmations, her brain began to restructure itself, strengthening the neural pathways associated with self-confidence, self-worth, and positivity.

Mel's newfound self-assurance radiated from within. She walked with a spring in her step, exuding a magnetic energy that drew people towards her. Friends and colleagues noticed the change, remarking on her newfound confidence and self-worth.

The power of positive affirmations went beyond Mel's personal life as she became more confident in pursuing her aspirations, speaking for herself, and embracing opportunities without hesitation.

She attracted mentors and collaborators who recognized her potential and supported her growth. Even setbacks and challenges no longer held the same power over her. Mel had cultivated a resilient mindset, embracing the belief that she could overcome any obstacle that came her way.

Action Steps

Here's a simple exercise to help you create your positive affirmations and incorporate them into your daily routine:

- Find a quiet and comfortable space to be alone with your thoughts. Take a few deep breaths to center yourself and create a sense of calm.

- Reflect on areas where you'd like to cultivate more positivity or self-confidence. It could be related to your work, relationships, personal growth, or any other aspect that resonates with you.

- Craft personalized affirmations by focusing on positive, empowering statements. For example, if you're working on self-confidence, you could say, "I am confident, capable, and worthy of success."

- Write down your affirmations in your journal. Use present tense and affirmations that feel authentic to you. Keep them concise and specific so they resonate deeply.

- Once you have your affirmations, find a quiet moment in your day to repeat them out loud or silently to yourself. You can do this in front of a mirror or during a moment of stillness and reflection. Repeat each affirmation several times, allowing positive energy to permeate your being.

As you continue practicing your affirmations daily, pay attention to any shifts in your mindset, emotions, and actions. Notice how they influence your thoughts and help you cultivate a more positive outlook.

Over time, feel free to adapt and evolve your affirmations as your needs and aspirations change. Tailor them to address new areas of growth and focus.

Remember, positive affirmations work best when practiced consistently and with genuine belief. They can be powerful tools to reprogram your mind, boost your self-esteem, and attract positivity. Embrace the journey of self-discovery and create affirmations that resonate with your unique desires and aspirations.

Going Beyond Ego to Embrace Interconnectedness and Self-Worth

The very essence of your existence goes back to when an egg attracted hundreds of sperm, and the chosen one with your unique DNA formed you. You are the result of an incredible cosmic lottery!

How does this relate to your self-worth? Let's talk about that. It's easy to fall into the trap of defining ourselves by our achievements, physical appearance, or what others think of us. However, the truth is that your worthiness comes from within. You are enough simply by existing. The fact that you are here right now makes you incredibly special.

When you think about it, things get fascinating. We are all stardust! The atoms that make up our bodies, such as carbon, oxygen, and nitrogen, were created in the ancient furnaces of stars through a process called nuclear fusion.[52] These star elements mixed and danced throughout the universe, eventually giving birth to our planet, Earth, and life. We are literally made of stardust, intricately woven into the vast cosmic tapestry.

The interconnectedness doesn't stop there. By understanding quantum physics, particles, atoms, and energy, we are all entangled in a complex web of interdependenc e.[53] Just like ecosystems, where the health of one species affects the entire system, we are all connected through this dance of energy and consciousness.

Quantum mechanics, which delves into the tiniest scales of matter and energy, reveals the phenomenon of entanglement. It states that particles interacting with each other remain connected regardless of the distance between them. This principle points to a universal interconnectivity that extends beyond our conventional understanding.

And speaking of ecosystems, they provide yet another example of interdependence. Ecosystems are complex networks of creatures, their habitats, and their interactions. Every organism within an ecosystem has a distinct purpose, and the well-being of one species can have a ripple effect on the entire system. It's a beautiful illustration of how interconnectedness permeates the natural world.

When we zoom out even further, evolutionary biology tells us that all living things, from bacteria to trees and large animals, share a common ancestor.[54] Our DNA ties us together, and scientists have made remarkable discoveries about our interconnectedness by studying the parallels and connections between species.

All matter in the universe, from galaxies to atoms, originated from the same source—the Big Bang.[55] Protons, neutrons, and electrons—the building blocks of everything—are part of this shared origin. We are connected to the cosmos on a fundamental level.

So, the idea of separation that the ego often clings to is false. You are so much more than just an anxious attachment style. You are a multidimensional person with dreams, passions, and talents waiting to be set free. You are stardust, convolutedly connected to the web of life, and part of something much bigger than yourself.

And here's another important realization: You existed before your partner and will continue to exist after any breakup. Take a moment to reconnect with your pre-relationship self. The same analogy applies to all other relationships in your life. Remember the hobbies, interests, and goals that brought you joy and made you feel alive. Rekindling those aspects of your identity can help you rediscover yourself outside the confines of the relationship.

We encourage you to embrace your cosmic origins, revel in your interconnectedness, and let your true self shine. You are matter in motion, a magnificent and unique expression of the universe. You are here for a reason, and your journey through life is an opportunity to explore, learn, and grow. So value yourself, practice positive affirmations, and embrace your interconnectedness with the cosmos. You are worthy of love; when you believe in your worth, you can form secure and fulfilling relationships. Trust in the stardust that flows through your veins and the incredible journey that has brought you here. You are more than you realize, and the world is waiting for you to shine your light.

Action Steps

Take a moment to remember your hobbies, interests, and aspirations. Grab a pen and paper and list the activities that bring you joy and ignite your passion. Then, set aside some dedicated time to reconnect with those activities. Place this in your planner or schedule! Whether painting, playing an instrument, running, or immersing yourself in a good book, indulge in those hobbies and rediscover the happiness they once brought you. Remind yourself that you can flourish alone. Embrace this opportunity for self-discovery and allow your true self to shine again.

The Role of Self-Care in Boosting Self-Esteem

Self-care routines are all the rage these days, and for good reason. They're not just about indulging in luxurious spa treatments or splurging on fancy bath products, though—it's about something much more profound. It's about showing yourself love and respect and, in turn, boosting your self-esteem. Engaging in activities that nourish your mind, body, and soul can do wonders in fostering self-love and a healthy sense of self-worth.

So, what exactly does self-care look like? It can take many forms, and finding what resonates with you is crucial. For some, it might mean carving out time in their day to journal their thoughts and emotions. Pouring your innermost thoughts onto paper can be incredibly therapeutic and a powerful way to connect with yourself. It allows you to process your feelings, gain clarity, and even discover new insights about yourself. It's like having a heartfelt conversation with your soul.

Others find solace in physical activities like yoga or strolls in the park. These simple acts of movement and being in nature can do wonders for your well-being. Yoga, with its focus on breath, mindfulness, and gentle movements, not only helps to strengthen your body but also cultivates a sense of inner peace and self-awareness. And let's not forget the healing power of nature. Walking amidst the trees, feeling the sun on your skin, and breathing in the fresh air can be incredibly rejuvenating. There is a formal name for this activity, and it's called forest bathing. Also known as "shinrin-yoku" in Japanese, this therapeutic practice reduces stress, boosts mood, and enhances overall health. You gain these benefits through your connection with nature but also through breathing in phytoncides (natural compounds released by trees) and soaking up nature's negative ions, which are abundant in forested areas.[56]

Self-care isn't a one-size-fits-all approach—it's a profoundly personal journey. Lorenzo, a 42-year-old man from Brazil, discovered his unique form of self-care: cooking. For Lorenzo, spending time in the kitchen, experimenting with flavors, and creating delicious meals has become his sanctuary. It's a way for him to express himself creatively, nurture his body with wholesome food, and, most importantly, enhance his self-worth.

Cooking has become his self-love ritual, reminding him that he can create something beautiful and nourishing, not just for others but for himself as well.

We encourage you to develop your personalized self-care toolkit that supports your emotional well-being and helps you foster self-love. We will explore how to do that next. Before we get to that, we must remind you of something important. Self-care is not selfish—it's essential. By nourishing your well-being, you are better equipped to show up fully in the world and be there for others.

Action Steps

Here's a simple activity to help you make your emotional self-care toolkit:

- Grab a pen and a notebook, or open a blank document on your computer.

- Reflect on activities or practices that bring joy, comfort, and emotional well-being. These can be journaling, meditation, listening to music, taking a bath, practicing mindfulness, engaging in a creative hobby, or any other activity that resonates with you.

- Write down a list of these activities in your notebook or document. Be specific, including any necessary materials or instructions for each activity.

- Consider the resources or tools you might need. For example, if you enjoy coloring as a stress relief, gather coloring books and colored pencils or markers.

- Once you have your list and any necessary resources, gather them in a designated space or container, such as a basket, a box, or any container that suits your preference.

- Decorate or personalize your toolkit if desired. You can add stickers, inspirational quotes, or other elements that make it visually appealing and inviting.

- Keep your emotional self-care toolkit in a readily accessible place, such as your nightstand, desk, or shelf, so you can easily access it whenever you need a moment of self-care.

- Refer to your toolkit if you need to practice self-care or boost your emotional well-being. Choose an activity that resonates with you in that moment and engage in it mindfully, allowing yourself to immerse in the experience fully.

Feel free to adapt and update your emotional self-care toolkit as your needs and preferences change.

Setting and Achieving Personal Goals: A Boost for Self-Worth

Setting and achieving personal goals can be a game-changer when boosting your self-esteem. Think about it. When you specify an objective, work toward it, and accomplish it, the feeling of accomplishment that washes over you is like a warm embrace. It's a validation of your abilities and a reminder that you can do great things.

There is a common misconception that goals must be tremendous, like climbing Mount Everest or writing a bestselling novel. But here's the thing—small goals matter, too. Finishing a book that has been collecting dust on your shelf or learning a new recipe can have a surprisingly positive impact on your self-esteem. It's about the satisfaction of completing something, no matter the size.

The science behind feelings of accomplishment, even when completing small tasks, lies in the brain's reward system.[57] When we set goals and accomplish them, our brain releases dopamine, a neurotransmitter associated with pleasure and reward. This surge of dopamine creates a sense of satisfaction and reinforces the behavior that led to the accomplishment. It activates the brain's circuitry responsible for motivation, learning, and positive emotions, boosting self-esteem.

Mila, a 26-year-old woman from Germany, sets weekly goals for herself, whether completing a challenging work project, trying out a new hobby, or allowing herself extra time to rest. By accomplishing these goals, she feels a sense of fulfillment and pride.

Just like Mila has done, it is noteworthy for you to set and accomplish small tasks for several reasons regularly. Firstly, minor duties provide a sense of progress and forward momentum in our lives. They break down larger goals into manageable steps, making them less overwhelming and more attainable. By consistently accomplishing these smaller tasks, we build a track record of success, which boosts our confidence and self-belief.

Secondly, regularly experiencing the feeling of accomplishment, even from small tasks, reinforces a positive mindset and motivates us to keep going.[58] It creates a positive feedback loop where each achievement fuels our motivation to tackle the next task. This cycle of setting and accomplishing goals cultivates a sense of purpose, fulfillment, and satisfaction in our lives.[59]

Additionally, setting small goals allows us to practice essential skills such as planning, organization, time management, and perseverance. These skills are transferable to larger goals and can significantly contribute to our personal and professional growth.

Regularly accomplishing small tasks also helps to build resilience and adaptability.[60] It teaches us to navigate challenges, overcome obstacles, and learn from setbacks. This resilience becomes invaluable when faced with more significant challenges or unexpected changes.

No matter how small, this feeling of accomplishment contributes to our overall well-being and happiness. It brings a sense of pride, self-worth, and fulfillment. By regularly setting and achieving small tasks, we create a pattern of positive experiences that contribute to our overall positive outlook on life.

This discussion would only be complete by discussing the difference between external and internal happiness. External happiness is tied to circumstances or possessions. It can come from getting a promotion, buying a new car, or taking a luxurious vacation. These experiences can bring temporary joy and release dopamine, the "feel-good" chemical in our brains. But here's the catch—they depend on external factors that can be fleeting.

On the other hand, internal happiness is a state of being that comes from within. It's about finding contentment and peace, regardless of external circumstances. It's the happiness that stays with you even during challenging times. Internal happiness is not reliant on achievements or material possessions but on cultivating a sense of equanimity.

Equanimity is maintaining a balanced and calm state of mind, regardless of what is happening around you. It's about being securely grounded within yourself rather than anxiously attached to external outcomes or validation. When you cultivate equanimity, you become less swayed by the ups and downs of life. Instead, you find a deep sense of peace, which becomes the foundation for your long-term happiness.

Action Steps

- Try this unique exercise to cultivate internal happiness and equanimity:
- Find a quiet and comfortable space where you can sit undisturbed for a few minutes.
- Close your eyes and take a few deep breaths, allowing yourself to relax and release any tension.
- Visualize a serene and peaceful place in your mind. It could be a lush forest, a tranquil beach, or any location that brings you a sense of calm and contentment.
- As you imagine yourself in this peaceful place, focus on your breath. With each inhale, imagine breathing in positivity, joy, and contentment. With each exhale, release any negativity, stress, or

worries.

- Now, in your mind's eye, start to notice and appreciate the small moments of beauty and joy around you in this imagined place. It could be the sound of birds chirping, the warmth of sunlight on your skin, or the gentle rustling of leaves.

- Allow yourself to fully immerse in these pleasant sensations and soak in the happiness they bring. Feel gratitude for these simple moments of beauty, and let them fill your heart with joy.

- Stay in this state of internal happiness for a few more breaths, savoring the feelings of contentment and peace.

- When you're ready, slowly open your eyes and carry this sense of internal happiness throughout your day.

Regularly practicing this exercise trains your mind to focus on the present moment, appreciate the beauty around you, and cultivate internal happiness. It serves as a gentle reminder to find joy in the simple things and to nurture a positive mindset.

Building Emotional Resilience

Weathering Life's Storms

∞

Born on July 12, 1997, in Mingora, Pakistan, Malala Yousafzai[61] is a name that resonates with courage, resilience, and the unwavering fight for education and equality. From a young age, Malala showed a passion for learning and a strong belief in the power of education. Growing up in the Swat Valley, she witnessed the oppressive rule of the Taliban, who sought to restrict girls' access to education. Undeterred, Malala became an outspoken advocate for girls' education, defying the oppressive regime and fearlessly voicing her opinions.

In 2009, at 11, Malala began anonymously writing a blog for BBC Urdu, documenting her experiences and advocating for girls' rights to education. Through her powerful words, she shed light on the dire situation in her hometown and the struggles girls who sought an education faced. Her blog gained international attention, and Malala's voice became a beacon of hope for millions worldwide.

However, tragedy struck on October 9, 2012, when a Taliban gunman boarded her school bus and targeted her for her activism. Malala was shot in the head, an act intended to silence her voice and suppress her fight. But little did they know that Malala's spirit was indomitable.

Miraculously surviving the attack, Malala's story garnered global attention and support. Her unwavering commitment to education and gender equality resonated with people from all walks of life. The world stood united in admiration of her bravery, and she became a symbol of resilience and the unyielding pursuit of justice.

As Malala recovered, her determination only grew stronger. She emerged as a global advocate, traveling the world and speaking on various platforms to address the importance of education, particularly for girls in marginalized communities. In 2013, at just 16 years old, she delivered a powerful speech at the United Nations, passionately advocating for every child's right to education.

Malala's advocacy work did not stop there. In 2014, she co-authored her memoir, I Am Malala, which became an international bestseller. The book chronicled her journey, her fight for education, and the challenges she faced along the way. It served as a testament to her unwavering spirit and inspired countless individuals to take a stand for education and equality.

In recognition of her remarkable efforts, Malala was awarded the Nobel Peace Prize in 2014, becoming the youngest-ever recipient of this prestigious honor. The award further amplified her message and brought global attention to the urgent need for education reform.

Today, Malala continues to make a profound impact. She co-founded the Malala Fund, which advocates for girls' education and empowers young girls to become change-makers in their communities. Through tireless efforts, she has helped millions of girls access quality education, breaking down barriers and opening doors to a brighter future.

In a world filled with challenges and adversities, the story of Malala Yousafzai stands as a shining testament to the power of resilience. Her remarkable journey from being a young girl defying the Taliban's oppressive regime to becoming a global advocate for education and equality showcases the unwavering strength of the human spirit. But resilience is not a quality reserved for the extraordinary; it is a trait inherent in us all. We can draw inspiration from Malala's story and learn how to cultivate our mental fortitude so we can overcome obstacles and thrive in the face of adversity.

Understanding Emotional Resilience

At its core, resilience is the ability to bounce back from setbacks, adapt, and persevere in pursuing our goals. Our inner strength allows us to face challenges head-on, even when the odds seem insurmountable.

We have seen what it means to have resilience in the face of peculiar odds like Malala, but what does this look like in everyday life? Resilience in daily life is about staying focused and determined when faced with challenges. It means not letting setbacks knock you down but seeing them as opportunities to learn and grow. Instead of getting overwhelmed, you roll up your sleeves and find creative ways to overcome obstacles. Try this imagery on for size: You're faced with a mountain of work that seems impossible to conquer. Instead of crawling under your desk in defeat, you whip out your superhero cape (or maybe your most beloved power suit) and channel your inner well of resourceful ingenuity.

Resilience also means keeping things in perspective and managing stress effectively. It's about realizing that tough times are temporary and that you have the power to take care of yourself and find healthy ways to cope. Whether practicing mindfulness, exercising, or seeking support from loved ones, you take steps to keep your stress levels in check.

On a day-to-day basis, resilience is about having a positive attitude and flipping negative thoughts on their head. It's like turning lemons into lemonade and finding the bright side of challenging situations. Resilient people focus on their strengths and accomplishments, celebrating progress rather than dwelling on failures.

Being resilient also means being adaptable and flexible. Life is full of unexpected twists and turns, and resilience helps you roll with the punches. It's about being open to change, letting go of rigid plans when necessary, and embracing new opportunities with an open mind.

Resilience is not a solo journey; it's about building a support system and leaning on others when needed. It's like having a safety net of people who believe in you and lift you up. Cultivating meaningful relationships and seeking guidance, encouragement, and companionship from trusted friends and family play a crucial role in resilience.

Malala drew strength from the love and encouragement of her family, and she sought solace and inspiration from the global community that rallied behind her cause. Surrounding yourself with people who uplift you, believe in your potential, and provide a safe space to share your fears and vulnerabilities is paramount to building mental fortitude. When we have a spirit of togetherness, we can weather the storms that life throws our way and emerge stronger on the other side.

It would have been easy for Malala to give up her cause when attacked. The world would have understood. But as a resilient being, she dared to keep going. You have to do the same, even when you're afraid or uncertain. Resilience means taking risks, stepping out of your comfort zone, and believing in yourself. Resilient individuals don't let fear of failure hold them back; instead, they see it as a stepping stone to success.

Maybe you don't have the traits of resilience highlighted above... yet. But it is not out of your reach. Building that type of mental fortitude, like any skill, requires practice and intentional effort. It starts with developing self-awareness. Understanding your strengths, weaknesses, and triggers empowers you to navigate challenges more effectively. By recognizing our thinking and behavior patterns, we can proactively address negative thought patterns and develop healthier coping strategies.

Moreover, resilience is intertwined with optimism and a growth mindset. Embracing a positive outlook, even in the face of adversity, will fuel your determination and help you find opportunities and challenges.

Action Steps

We started this chapter with Malala's because we understand that having role models who exemplify resilience is essential. They provide us with tangible proof that overcoming adversity is possible. When we see someone who has faced and triumphed over challenges perhaps similar to ours, it sparks a sense of hope and belief in our ability to persevere. Role models serve as a source of inspiration, guiding us through difficult times by showing us practical strategies, positive mindsets, and the strength to bounce back from setbacks. They offer a roadmap for building resilience and remind us that we are not alone in our struggles, instilling the confidence and motivation to navigate our hardships with determination and courage.

Here is an exercise to help you find role models that empower you to overcome stress and hardship:

1. Reflect on your values and the qualities you admire: Take a moment to think about the values that are important to you and the qualities you admire in others. Consider traits like resilience, perseverance, determination, and optimism.

2. Identify potential role models: Make a list of individuals who embody these qualities and have successfully overcome challenges. These role models can be well-known figures or people in your immediate circle, such as family members, friends, or mentors.

3. Research their stories: Dive deeper into the stories of your chosen role models. Look for biogra-

phies, books, interviews, articles, or videos that highlight their journeys and how they navigated through tough times. Please pay attention to the strategies and mindsets they employ to overcome adversity.

4. Extract lessons and inspiration: As you learn about their experiences, extract the lessons and inspiration that resonate most with you. Take note of their specific actions, attitudes, or approaches to overcome stress and hardship. These can serve as valuable insights and guidance for your journey.

5. Apply their wisdom to your life: Finally, consider how you can apply the knowledge of your chosen role models to your own life. Reflect on their strategies and see how to incorporate them into your approach to stress and hardship. It could be adopting a positive mindset, seeking support, setting goals, or developing resilience-building practices.

Remember that while role models can provide valuable guidance and inspiration, your journey is ultimately unique. Adapt the lessons you learn from your role models to suit your circumstances and personal growth.

The Connection Between Emotional Resilience and Anxious Attachment

Anxiety and how well we can handle challenging situations strongly connect with anxious attachment. Having high emotional resilience is like having a secret weapon against the anxiety that often comes with the attachment style.

Emotional resilience protects us from the adverse effects of all the stress and anxiety we experience because of anxious attachment. Emotional resilience makes us better at handling our emotions. We gain the ability to regulate them more effectively, which means we can dial down the intensity of our reactions when we perceive threats in our relationships.

Prio is a talented professional working in a fast-paced environment in Trinidad. Prio tends to get anxious at work, often worrying excessively about his colleagues' opinions, performance, and the potential for rejection or failure.

One day, Prio receives feedback on a project from his supervisor that is less positive than he had hoped. Immediately, he feels a surge of anxiety and self-doubt creeping in. However, having taken a course on emotional regulation techniques, Prio knows he doesn't have to let the situation get the better of him.

First, Prio takes a moment to acknowledge his anxious feelings without judgment. He recognizes that his anxious attachment style might exacerbate his reaction to the feedback. By accepting his emotions, he creates the space to respond more thoughtfully.

Next, Prio engages in a calming strategy he learned to regulate his emotions. He closes his eyes, takes a few deep breaths, and recites positive affirmations to himself. Taking this moment to himself helps him calm his racing thoughts and bring his focus back to the present moment.

Prio then challenges his anxious thoughts by reframing the situation. Instead of viewing the feedback as a personal failure, he reminds himself that constructive criticism is an opportunity for growth and improvement. He reframes the feedback as valuable input that can help him refine his skills and deliver even better results in the future.

Feeling more centered and in control, Prio has a follow-up conversation with his supervisor. Instead of dwelling on his anxiety or seeking constant reassurance, he confidently approaches the discussion and is willing to learn. He asks for specific areas of improvement, seeks clarification on expectations, and discusses strategies for addressing the feedback constructively.

Emotional regulation is a valuable tool for managing anxious attachment tendencies in all areas of life. Imagine you're dealing with a situation that triggers your anxiety: Maybe your partner is busy and hasn't texted you back, and your mind starts racing, thinking they're losing interest. With higher emotional resilience, you can take a step back, take a deep breath, and assess the situation more calmly. You can challenge those anxious thoughts and choose a more balanced response rather than spiraling into panic or pushing your partner away.

Building emotional resilience is like giving yourself an emotional safety net. It helps you bounce back from setbacks and challenges in your relationships. It doesn't mean you won't feel anxious at times, but it equips you with the tools to handle those feelings healthily.

Mindfulness is a powerful tool that helps you build emotional regulation as it cultivates self-awareness and present-moment attention. By practicing mindfulness activities like meditation, deep breathing, and grounding, you develop the ability to observe your thoughts, emotions, and bodily sensations without judgment or reactivity. This ability to observe is also a result of you becoming more attuned to your internal experiences in real-time. Additionally, mindfulness helps create a mental space between what's triggering you (the stimulus) and your response so you can choose how you react to emotional triggers rather than automatically reacting.

Journal Prompts

Take a few moments to think about a recent situation where you felt a strong emotional reaction. It could be a moment of frustration, anxiety, or even joy. Reflect on how you responded to that emotion. Did you react impulsively, or were you able to pause and respond in a more controlled manner? What strategies did you use to regulate your feelings in that moment? Consider how you can further develop your emotional regulation skills to better navigate similar situations in the future.

Building Emotional Resilience: Techniques and Strategies

Life can throw some serious curveballs, like that unexpected pop quiz or when you realize you're out of coffee. Building emotional resilience is what allows you to bounce back better than ever. Remember when we said that building resilience is a skill anyone can develop? It's like going to the gym and working to build physical muscles. Build your mental muscles by implementing the following workout techniques:

Exercise 1: Self-Care Recharge

Start by giving yourself a big, warm hug. Take time to recharge those batteries and indulge in activities that make you feel good. It could be a luxurious bubble bath, a refreshing walk in nature, or even a guilt-free binge-watching session of your favorite show. Think of self-care as a bit of vacation for your soul, replenishing your emotional reserves and providing a fresh perspective to face any challenge.

Exercise 2: Reframing Reps

When life hands you lemons, instead of pouting about the sour taste, ask yourself, "What can I learn from this? How can I grow stronger?" Find those silver linings and embrace the valuable lessons that come with every challenge. Setbacks can be stepping stones to success if you see them that way.

Exercise 3: Support Network Squats

Surround yourself with uplifting people who have your back. They're like your emotional cheerleaders, ready to boost your spirits and remind you that you're not alone. Reach out to those friends who always make you laugh or that family member who gives the best pep talks. They'll be there to lend a listening ear or join you in a good old-fashioned venting session. Don't forget it's okay to lean on others for support.

Exercise 4: Positive Thinking Push-Ups

Engage the cheerleader squad in your head. Challenge those negative thoughts and replace them with positive and empowering ones. Instead of dwelling on what went wrong, focus on what you can do to improve things. It's like flipping a switch that illuminates the path forward, no matter how dim it may seem.

Exercise 5: Flexibility Flow

Embrace the beauty of flexibility as you navigate life's roller coaster ride. Sometimes, things don't go according to plan, but that's okay. Being emotionally resilient means being adaptable and going with the flow. Imagine yourself doing the salsa when life throws you a curveball, gracefully moving with the rhythm instead of freezing like a deer in headlights. Embrace the unexpected and trust in your ability to handle whatever comes your way.

The Journey to Security

Embracing a New Attachment Style

∞

We start this chapter differently than the rest with a fun activity. It's an attachment art exercise we call "Creating Your Attachment Tree." You will need simple materials: a piece of blank paper or canvas, colored markers, crayons, colored pencils or paints, and your imagination. Then follow these instructions:

1. **Select Your Artistic Medium:** Choose your preferred art supplies. Whether you're an avid painter, a doodler, or a fan of colorful markers, pick the materials that resonate with you.

2. **Set the Scene:** Find a comfortable and quiet space to focus on your artwork without distractions. Create a relaxed atmosphere with your favorite music, lighting, or a warm beverage.

3. **Visualize Your Attachment Tree:** Imagine you

are an artist, and your task is to depict your attachment journey as a tree. This tree will symbolize your relationships, experiences, and emotions related to attachment throughout your life.

4. **Start with the Roots:** Begin by drawing the roots of your attachment tree. These represent your earliest attachment experiences, such as childhood relationships with caregivers, family, and close friends.

5. **Branch Out:** As you move up from the roots, draw branches representing significant relationships and experiences from different life stages. Use different colors or patterns to reflect the emotions associated with each branch.

6. **Attach Memories and Feelings:** Along the branches, add leaves, flowers, or fruits. Each represents specific memories, feelings, or moments related to your attachments. Don't be afraid to get creative with your symbolism.

7. **Express Yourself:** Feel free to use words, quotes, or phrases that capture the essence of your attachment experiences. Write them on or around the tree to give your artwork a voice.

8. **Reflect and Connect:** Take a step back and ad-

mire your Attachment Tree. What do you notice? Are there patterns, colors, or shapes that surprise you? Reflect on the emotions that arise as you look at your creation.

9. **Share Your Story:** This step is optional. If you're comfortable, you can share your Attachment Tree with your partner, a trusted friend, or a therapist. Explaining the symbolism behind your artwork can be a powerful way to open up about your attachment experiences.

10. **Keep Your Tree**: Display your Attachment Tree somewhere you can see it daily. It's a visual reminder of your attachment journey, the beauty of your growth, and the ways you will continue to branch out.

There's no right or wrong way to create your Attachment Tree. This exercise is all about self-expression and reflection. Have fun, and let your creativity flow as you explore your attachment experiences through art!

This exercise serves as a foundation for our upcoming exploration of secure attachment. It helps you identify where you currently stand in your attachment journey. This understanding will make it easier for you to grasp the principles and practices that lead to secure attachments. Ultimately, it will help you build more fulfilling and meaningful relationships.

Understanding Secure Attachment

Secure attachment is about feeling at ease in both solitude and your relationships. It's like having a well-constructed house in a lively neighborhood. This house represents your sense of security, while the neighborhood symbolizes the world and your connections with others.

With secure attachment, you're not isolating yourself inside your house, nor are you desperately holding onto anyone who comes your way. Instead, your home is solidly built, allowing you to explore the neighborhood confidently.

In a securely attached state, you find comfort in your company (solitude) and interactions with others (relationships). You don't need to build walls to keep people out, nor do you leave your doors wide open for just anyone. You strike a balanced approach.

In contrast to anxious attachment, where fear of abandonment can leave you feeling unstable, secure attachment is akin to having a house built on solid ground. You have faith that your home will endure, and you can depend on the support provided by your relationships without constant worry.

Psychologist Mary Ainsworth's "Strange Situation" study gives us a glimpse into securely attached children's behavior.[62] They're like explorers who venture out into the neighborhood, knowing they have a safe, welcoming house (their caregiver) to return to whenever they need to refuel and rest.

You're not born with secure attachment, like the house itself. It's more like carefully constructing and maintaining your home over time. You build it through healthy experiences, supportive relationships, and self-reflection.

Building a secure attachment style is a journey, much like transforming a fixer-upper into a comfortable, inviting home. It requires self-awareness to understand your needs, emotional growth to strengthen your foundations, and a commitment to nurturing healthy relationships to ensure your house (your sense of security) remains a welcoming and dependable place in the vibrant neighborhood of life.

To be classified as having a secure attachment, you must exhibit these traits:

- **Trust and Security:** You genuinely believe in yourself and others. You trust that someone will meet your needs, and you will feel confident in your relationships, even when facing tough times. For instance, when you encounter a challenging situation, you trust that your partner will support you and are not afraid to be vulnerable with them.

- **Emotional Availability:** You're comfortable with emotions, both yours and others. You listen, understand, and empathetically respond when someone shares their feelings with you.

- **Healthy Balance Between Independence & Interdependence:** You balance having your own life and nurturing your relationships. You don't depend on others for validation but appreciate your loved ones.

- **Effective Compassionate Communication:** You excel in communication. You express your needs and listen actively to others. You believe in open and honest communication, which helps you resolve conflicts constructively.

- **Emotional Regulation:** You handle your emotions well, knowing your triggers and coping mechanisms. You avoid extreme reactions and don't let emotions overwhelm you.

- **Positive Self-Image:** You have a healthy sense of self-worth and trust in your abilities. You believe you're worthy of love and support and see the best in others.

- **Toughness and Adaptability:** You're resilient in your relationships, dealing with change, conflict, and growth. You're open to new experiences and feedback and are always willing to learn and adapt.

- **Reality Checking:** You question anxious thoughts, seeking evidence and alternative explanations. You replace catastrophic thinking with a more realistic perspective.

- **Healthy Coping Mechanisms:** When faced with anxiety or fear, you turn to healthy coping activities like relaxation, self-care, or engaging in enjoyable hobbies.

- **Balanced Perspective:** You understand that anxiety and fear are expected, and you don't exaggerate potential outcomes. Instead, you focus on problem-solving and finding constructive solutions to challenges.

Have you ever seen these characteristics in yourself? Maybe you've had moments when you felt secure in your relationships or handled challenging situations with confidence. Remember, you're not limited to just one attachment style; you can change and grow with some effort and self-awareness.

If you don't recognize these traits in yourself, don't worry. You're reading this to develop these skills. Take a deep breath; you're exactly where you should be. Keep moving forward; someday, you'll notice how you've evolved when you revisit this.

The words we choose significantly impact how we see ourselves and the world around us. When we used "you" to describe the qualities of secure attachment, we did it to help you imagine and connect with the idea of being someone who possesses these qualities.

Think of it like this: when you read those words and see "you," it's like looking in a mental mirror and seeing yourself as a person with secure attachment traits. This mental picture can help you reshape your thoughts and feelings about yourself.

Visualization is like practicing for a role in a play. By repeatedly seeing yourself as someone with secure attachment qualities, you're more likely to act in ways that reflect those qualities in your real-life relationships. So, reading and imagining these traits in yourself can help you become more secure in your attachments over time. It's like setting a positive intention for how you want to be in your relationships.

Action Steps

Let's build upon the exercise with which we started this chapter with this visualization exercise:

1. Find a quiet and comfortable space where you

won't be disturbed. Take a few deep breaths and allow yourself to relax.

2. Close your eyes and imagine yourself standing in a beautiful garden. Picture vibrant flowers, tall trees, and a gentle breeze.

3. Visualize a solid and sturdy tree in the center of the garden. This tree represents your secure attachment base.

4. As you approach the tree, feel its solid presence and the warmth it radiates. Place your hand on the trunk and feel the texture of the bark. This tree is your haven, always there to provide support and comfort.

5. Take a moment to reflect on the relationships in your life. Visualize the people who are important to you, such as family, friends, or a partner. See them as colorful, beautiful flowers blooming around the tree.

6. As you observe the flowers, notice how each represents a different secure attachment aspect. Some flowers symbolize trust, others represent reliability, and some embody emotional support.

7. Appreciate each flower's unique qualities and

their role in your attachment journey. Visualize the connections between the flowers and the tree, representing your bond and security in these relationships.

8. Finally, embrace the feeling of being supported by the tree and surrounded by the vibrant, nurturing flowers. Allow yourself to feel safe, confident, and loved in this visualization.

9. When you're ready, slowly open your eyes and take a few more deep breaths, carrying the sense of secure attachment and connection with you into your day.

This visualization exercise is a tool to help you cultivate a sense of secure attachment. Feel free to modify it to suit your preferences and make it even more personal.

From Anxious to Secure: The Transformation Process

To learn a secure attachment style, you must undergo the process of unlearning anxious attachment. Unlearning and relearning might sound like a complex process, but in reality, it's something your brain does all the time.[63] Think of your brain as a vast library filled with books of knowledge and habits. Sometimes, you realize that a book on the shelf isn't quite right, is outdated, or doesn't serve you well anymore. That's when the unlearning process begins.

When you decide to unlearn something, your brain takes that outdated book off the shelf and examines it closely. It starts to identify the parts that need changing or replacing. Unlearning might involve breaking down old habits or beliefs that no longer make sense. Just like updating a book with new information or better ideas, your brain replaces the old with the new.

As you unlearn, your brain strengthens new neural connections. These new connections represent the relearning process. Your brain adapts to fresh information, skills, or perspectives, just like you'd absorb the contents of a new, improved book.

As smooth as it sounds in theory, this process can be challenging because your brain initially resists change (it loves the familiar!). Still, with patience and practice, you gradually reshape your mental landscape.

Understanding this process allows you to see that relearning your attachment style is precisely that—a process. Transitioning from an anxious attachment style to a secure one is a journey, not simply flipping a switch. The course unfolds over time with its own hills and valleys, much like learning a new language or mastering a musical instrument.

Becoming more securely attached involves adopting the characteristics of this identity. The gradual change requires patience and a growth mindset—a belief in your capacity to change and grow. This mindset extends to both yourself and your relationships.

Feeling safe and protected within yourself is a cornerstone of secure attachment. It involves having a positive self-image and trusting in your abilities and the worthiness of love and support. When you feel secure within, you can offer and receive love in a healthier, more fulfilling way.

Feeling secure within the world is equally vital. It means understanding that the world is not an inherently threatening place. Securely attached individuals have faith in the goodwill and intentions of those around them, which fosters a sense of safety and belonging.

To aid in this voyage, practicing gratitude and appreciation is beneficial. Gratitude helps shape positive narratives in our relationships, emphasizing the good and the supportive aspects. Encourage yourself to find and express gratitude for your partner and your relationship, fostering a sense of connection and mutual appreciation.

Journal Prompts

Use the following journal prompt to help mold your brain to align with secure attachment. Write a letter to yourself from the perspective of a secure attachment figure writing to you. Picture this figure as someone who radiates confidence, trust, and unwavering support, especially during uncertainty or self-doubt.

Think about what this secure attachment figure would say to reassure and uplift you when the world feels uncertain and your confidence wavers. What kind of advice, guidance, or comforting words of encouragement would they lovingly offer to help you navigate through challenging times? Imagine their compassionate tone and empathetic understanding as they address your concerns and insecurities.

But don't stop there; this exercise goes beyond the act of writing. Reflect on how you can internalize and embody these messages of secure attachment in your everyday life. Consider the practical steps you can take to integrate these reassuring thoughts and empowering beliefs into your daily experiences and interactions.

Perhaps, in this process, you'll discover new ways to boost your self-confidence, foster trust in your relationships, or find solace in moments of vulnerability. Maybe you'll uncover strategies to balance your independence with your need for connection, just as a securely attached person would.

By immersing yourself in the roles of both the writer and the receiver of this letter, we hope you can tap into the reservoir of security and support within you. This immersion will help strengthen your sense of well-being and ability to navigate life's challenges with a more secure and resilient mindset.

Practical Steps Towards Secure Attachment

Do you remember Marika from the introduction of this book? Anxious attachment casts a shadow over her relationship with her significant other and her other connections. Something had to give, and eventually, she found the courage to seek the help of a therapist. She opened up with this person, and together, they formulated a plan to help Marika attach more securely. Armed with a newfound determination, she set out on her journey toward a more secure attachment style, using these actionable steps as her guide:

Grounding Techniques

Marika began by practicing grounding techniques to manage her anxiety. Whenever she felt that familiar wave of anxiety washing over her, she took deep breaths, reminding herself to stay present. This simple act helped her regain control over her racing thoughts and emotions.

Letting Go of Judgments

She consciously worked on releasing judgments, especially regarding Alan's actions and words. Instead of labeling his behaviors as "good" or "bad," she reminded herself that people are complex and their actions may not always reflect their feelings. This shift in perspective allowed her to approach their interactions with more understanding and empathy. She transferred this way of thinking to her other dealings as well.

Effective Communication

Marika realized the importance of effective communication in building healthier relationships. Instead of making assumptions, she listened actively and asked Alan what was going on when she felt uncertain or anxious. This open dialogue helped bridge the gap between them, fostering a deeper connection.

In addition, Marika learned to communicate her needs assertively. Instead of passive-aggressive remarks, she practiced expressing her feelings openly and directly. For instance, when she felt disconnected from Alan, she would say, "I feel lonely when I don't get to spend quality time with you. Can we plan some time together this week?" This approach allowed her to address her needs without creating unnecessary tension.

Embracing Uncertainty

One of the most challenging steps for Marika was accepting that she couldn't control everything or predict the future. She was proactive about letting go of her need for constant reassurance and began to trust in herself and the strength of her relationships.

Self-Work

Marika focused on building her self-esteem and self-confidence to build a strong sense of self-worth. She practiced positive self-talk daily, acknowledging her strengths and celebrating her accomplishments, no matter how small. Self-care became a priority; she dedicated time to activities that brought her joy and relaxation.

Over time, Marika's efforts paid off. She noticed a shift in her attachment style from anxious to more secure. The trust she had built within herself and her relationship with Alan allowed her to find peace and security in their love. Marika's journey wasn't without its challenges, but with determination and the right tools, she transformed her attachment style, bringing harmony and happiness into her life and relationships.

Following similar action steps, anyone, including you, can follow a path similar to Marika's in achieving a more secure attachment style. It all starts with self-awareness and a commitment to personal growth.

Embracing the Journey: The Road to Secure Attachment

The journey toward achieving a secure attachment style is not just about reaching a destination; it's a metamorphosis that occurs as you navigate the intricate landscape of emotions and relationships. This journey is marked by milestones such as learning to trust yourself and others. Along the way, you will have to break down the walls built around your heart and gradually rebuild bridges of trust that connect you to those you care about.

Embracing vulnerability, as eloquently explained by renowned researcher and author Brené Brown in her TED talk on the power of vulnerability,[64] is at the heart of this transformation. Understanding that vulnerability isn't a sign of weakness but a strength that allows you to authentically connect with others and yourself.

As you embark on this path of self-discovery and growth, we encourage you to embrace the possibilities that lie ahead. Consider the opportunity to leave a positive legacy in your relationships—a legacy defined by trust, security, and deeper connections. You are now evolving into a person with a secure attachment style, and every day, week, and month presents an opportunity for growth and self-improvement. We've helped you take the first steps toward a better future, and the rest is up to you.

To support you on your path, we invite you to explore our website (https://www.infinitecreationsinc.com/), which is filled with additional practices and exercises to help you maintain and strengthen your secure attachment style and healthy relationships.

To close this chapter and start your evolution, close your eyes and visualize a brighter, more secure future in your relationships. Imagine yourself in a secure, loving relationship where you feel safe and cherished. See yourself in dependable friendships and thriving in your professional exchanges. Don't exclude the vision of confidence in your interactions with strangers and acquaintances. Engage all five senses as you picture this future: the warmth of a hug, the trust in your partner's eyes, the sound of laughter, the taste of shared moments, and the scent of love in all its forms in the air. This is the destination you are striving for on your journey to secure attachment, and it's within your reach.

Conclusion

∞

That was a lot of information to digest. So, let's decompress together. Take a deep breath in, allowing your chest to rise as you inhale slowly. As you exhale, release any tension and uncertainty you carry within you. With each breath, acknowledge the fear of the unknown but remind yourself that you are brave enough to pursue the future that is rightfully yours. Inhale strength and exhale doubt, letting go of past attachment patterns that no longer serve you. Embrace the present moment, knowing that by nurturing your inner security, you are creating the foundation for healthier, more fulfilling relationships ahead.

As you begin this journey of self-transformation, be joyful that you are not starting from scratch. You are now working with knowledge that empowers your every step. From the very first page of this book, we have set you up with insights to provide a deeper understanding of what anxious attachment is and how it affects your relationships. You've learned to spot the behaviors that stem from it and the importance of coping mechanisms to deal with anxiety.

As you've flipped through the chapters, you've seen how trust plays a central role in conquering anxious attachment, and you've grasped the significance of setting healthy boundaries that help build secure relationships. The book has given you some fantastic techniques for recognizing and managing your triggers and ways to boost your self-esteem and build your emotional strength.

But beyond all these practical tips and exercises, this reading excursion has been about exploring yourself. You've peeled back the layers of your attachment style, and you're on a path toward having a more secure attachment style.

When you look back on what you've learned in each chapter, we hope that it's clear that this book has been all about nurturing happy and secure relationships with others and with yourself. In the end, we hope you've discovered that pursuing a secure attachment is closely tied to self-discovery and personal growth. By navigating your attachment style, you unravel the layers of your past to shape a more secure and fulfilling future.

As you reflect on your progress and growth throughout this book, from understanding anxious attachment to participating in the exercise and journal prompts outlined, we want you to recognize the power of patience and persistence. This is a journey that unfolds over time, and every small step you take is a meaningful stride toward building healthier connections.

Now, it's time for action! Start implementing the strategies and exercises we've discussed in your daily life. Remember, overcoming anxious attachment and fostering secure relationships is an ongoing process that requires consistent effort. Embrace the opportunities to practice, learn, and grow as you navigate this path.

As you continue your journey, don't hesitate to seek further resources, connect with support groups, or consider professional help if needed. Your commitment to personal growth and self-improvement extends far beyond these pages.

Overcoming anxious attachment is entirely possible. Believe in yourself, trust the process, and know you can create the meaningful connections you deserve.

Inspire Others: Leave a Transformative Review

As you finish *The Simple Path to Anxious Attachment Recovery*, your journey offers invaluable insights. Leaving a review becomes a lifeline for those wrestling with attachment issues, showing them they're not alone. More importantly, your review prompts action. It motivates others to begin their own healing journey to address their attachment challenges head-on.

In essence, your review isn't merely a reflection; it's a gift to those seeking their own path to healing and growth. By sharing your journey and the book's impact, you become a part of a larger community dedicated to positive change. You offer assurance to those in need, letting them know they can also find their way to more secure, fulfilling relationships. Your review becomes a beacon of light, a source of hope, and a catalyst for transformation.

Now, take a moment to share your experience wherever you acquired this book.

A meaningful review can be concise yet impactful. Reflect on how the book aided your journey, what transformation you've witnessed, and why others should embark on this path, too. Mention specific tools or insights that resonated with you.

Your review isn't just words; it's a catalyst for others' growth. You guide fellow seekers toward healthier relationships by sharing your story and insights. Your action today can inspire countless transformations. Leave your review now and light the path for others.

1. Katie, B. (2017, October 16). Four liberating questions — The work of Byron Katie. The Work of Byron Katie. https://thework.com/2017/10/four-liberating-questions/

2. Romantic Love Conceptualized as an Attachment Process (n.d.). University of Denver. https://www2.psych.ubc.ca/~schaller/Psyc591Readings/HazanShaver1987.pdf

3. Potential regulatory elements between attachment styles and psychopathology: Rejection sensitivity and self-esteem. (n.d.). PubMed Central (PMC). https://www.ncbi.nlm.nih.gov/pmc/articles/PMC6732807/

4. Mcleod, S. (n.d.). John Bowlby | Maternal deprivation theory. Study Guides for Psychology Students - Simply Psychology. https://www.simplypsychology.org/bowlby.html

5. Montijo, S. (n.d.). Relationships: Can you go from insecure to secure attachment style? Psych Central. https://psychcentral.com/lib/how-to-change-insecure-attachment-style

6. An attachment perspective on psychopathology. (n.d.). PubMed Central (PMC). https://www.ncbi.nlm.nih.gov/pmc/articles/PMC3266769/

7. The role ego plays in your personality. (2005, November 25). Verywell Mind. https://www.verywellmind.com/what-is-the-ego-2795167

8. Katie, B. (2017, October 16). Four liberating questions — The work of Byron Katie. The Work of Byron Katie. https://thework.com/2017/10/four-liberating-questions/

9. Feeney, J.A. and Noller, P. (1990) attachment style as a predictor of adult romantic relationships. Journal of personality and social psychology, 58, 281-291. - References - Scientific research publishing. (n.d.). SCIRP Open Access. https://www.scirp.org/(S(351jmbntvnsjt1aadkposzje))/reference/ReferencesPapers.aspx?ReferenceID=1235434

10. Self-fulfilling prophecies in social situations. (n.d.). Succeed Socially.com | Free Social Skills Guide For Adults. https://www.succeedsocially.com/selffulfillingprophecy

11. What is Codependency? (2020, August 31). Verywell Mind. https://www.verywellmind.com/what-is-codependency-5072124

12. How poetry can help kids develop reading skills - Reading partners | Reading partners. (2020, May 26). Reading Partners. https://readingpartners.org/blog/poetry-can-help-kids-develop-reading-skills/

13. Building a better brain through music, dance and poetry. (2023, April 3). NPR. https://www.npr.org/sections/health-shots/2023/04/03/1167494088/your-brain-on-art-music-dance-poetry

14. Holland, K. (n.d.). Identifying and managing abandonment issues. Healthline. https://www.healthline.com/health/mental-health/abandonment-issues

15. Traumatic stress: Effects on the brain. (n.d.) . PubMed Central (PMC). https://www.ncbi.nlm.nih.gov/pmc/articles/PMC3181836/

16. What is the fawning trauma response? (n.d.). Psychology Today. https://www.psychologytoday.com/intl/blog/emotional-sobriety/202303/what-is-the-fawning-trauma-response

17. Mindfulness-based interventions for anxiety and depression. (n.d.). PubMed Central (PMC). https://www.ncbi.nlm.nih.gov/pmc/articles/PMC5679245/

18. Emotional hypersensitivity: When emotions are always bursting. (2022, November 8). Exploring your mind. https://exploringyourmind.com/emotional-hypersensitivity-emotions-always-bursting/

19. The contribution of attachment styles and reassurance seeking to trust in romantic couples. (n.d.). PubMed Central (PMC). https://www.ncbi.nlm.nih.gov/pmc/articles/PMC8895702/

20. The process of idealization. (n.d.). Psychology Today. https://www.psychologytoday.com/us/blog/the-young-and-the-restless/201112/the-process-idealization

21. Idealization and devaluation as defense mechanisms in BPD. (2008, June 4). Verywell Mind. https://www.verywellmind.com/devaluation-and-idealization-in-bpd-425291

22. The biology of fear- and anxiety-related behaviors. (n.d.). PubMed Central (PMC). https://www.ncbi.nlm.nih.gov/pmc/articles/PMC3181681/

23. Adult attachment and happiness: Individual differences in the experience and consequences of positive emotions. (n.d.) Frontiers in Psychology. https://experienciasomaticauruguay.com/wp-content/uploads/2018/07/Attachment-style-predicts-affect-cognitive-apparaisals-and-social-functioning.pdf

24. Directing your destiny: How to become the writer, producer, and director of your dreams: Grace, Jennifer, Dyer, Serena: 9781401941871: Amazon.com : Books. (n.d.). Amazon.com. Spend less. Smile more. https://www.amazon.com/Directing-Your-Destiny-Producer-Director/dp/1401941877/

25. Measuring the effects of self-awareness: Construction of the self-awareness outcomes questionnaire. (n.d.). PubMed Central (PMC). https://www.ncbi.nlm.nih.gov/pmc/articles/PMC5114878/Measuring the effects of self-awareness: Construction of the self-awareness outcomes questionnaire. (n.d.) . PubMed Central (PMC). https://www.ncbi.nlm.nih.gov/pmc/articles/PMC5114878/

26. What is psychosynthesis? (2022, February 21). Institute of Psychosynthesis. https://www.psychosynthesis.org/about/what-is-psychosynthesis/

27. The positive effects of mindfulness on self-esteem. (n.d.). The Journal of Positive Psychology. https://psycnet.apa.org/record/2013-29305-002

28. Curtiss, Ph.D, Levine B.A., Ander, B.A., & Baker, Ph.D. (2021, June 17). Cognitive-Behavioral Treatments for Anxiety and Stress-Related Disorders. FOCUS: The Journal of Lifelong Learning in Psychiatry, Volume 19(Issue 2), 184–189. https://doi.org/10.1176/appi.focus.20200045

29. DiSanti. (n.d.). Understanding Nervines & Adaptogens: Herbs for Stress & the Nervous System. Understanding Nervines & Adaptogens: Herbs for Stress & the Nervous System. Retrieved September 11, 2023, from https://blog.mountainroseherbs.com/understanding-nervines-adaptogens

30. What is Bioenergetics? (n.d.). Lowen Foundation. https://www.lowenfoundation.org/what-is-bioenergetics

31. The role of self-compassion in development: A healthier way to relate to oneself. (n.d.). PubMed Central (PMC). https://www.ncbi.nlm.nih.gov/pmc/articles/PMC2790748/

32. The clinical characterization of the adult patient with an anxiety or related disorder aimed at personalization of management. (n.d.). PubMed Central (PMC). https://www.ncbi.nlm.nih.gov/pmc/articles/PMC8429350/

33. 6 new findings about millennials. (2020, December 14). Pew Research Center. https://www.pewresearch.org/short-reads/2014/03/07/6-new-findings-about-millennials/

34. COVID-19 pandemic triggers 25% increase in prevalence of anxiety and depression worldwide. (2022, March 2). World Health Organization (WHO). https://www.who.int/news/item/02-03-2022-covid-19-pandemic-triggers-25-increase-in-prevalence-of-anxiety-and-depression-worldwide

35. Effects of positive and negative childhood experiences on adult family health - PubMed. (2021, April 5). PubMed. https://doi.org/10.1186/s12889-021-10732-w

36. Influence of attachment styles on romantic relationships. (n.d.). Experts@Minnesota. https://experts.umn.edu/en/publications/influence-of-attachment-styles-on-romantic-relationships

37. Deschene, L. (2022, September 8). Letting go of attachment: From a to Zen. Tiny Buddha. https://tinybuddha.com/blog/letting-go-of-attachment-from-a-to-zen/

38. The difference between emotional boundaries and walls. (n.d.). https://facilitatoronfire.net/episode43/

39. *Peaceful parent, happy kids.* (n.d.). Google Books. https://books.google.com/books/about/Peaceful_Parent_Happy_Kids.html?id=EYQyoR-oqqAC

40. Two wolves. (2013, December 6). Virtues For Life. https://www.virtuesforlife.com/two-wolves/

41. Understanding the impact of trauma - trauma-informed care in behavioral health services - NCBI bookshelf. (n.d.). National Center for Biotechnology Information. https://www.ncbi.nlm.nih.gov/books/NBK207191/

42. *Membership in a devalued social group and emotional well-being: Developing a model of personal self-esteem, collective self-esteem, and group socialization.* (n.d.). SpringerLink. https://link.springer.com/article/10.1023/A:1021644225878

43. "It's all in your head": Managing catastrophizing before it becomes a catastrophe. (n.d.). PubMed Central (PMC). https://www.ncbi.nlm.nih.gov/pmc/articles/PMC8525530/

44. Schneider, N. (2020, December 3). NLP technique for anxiety: Superman. Global NLP Training Blog. https://www.globalnlptraining.com/blog/nlp-technique-for-anxiety-superman/

45. Breathing to reduce stress. (n.d.). Better Health Channel - Better Health Channel. https://www.betterhealth.vic.gov.au/health/healthyliving/breathing-to-reduce-stress

46. Øinæs, J. (2023, May 29). The law of one explained. Wisdom from North. https://wisdomfromnorth.com/the-law-of-one-explained/

47. Research shows majority of women struggle with self esteem. (n.d.). Startups Magazine. https://startupsmagazine.co.uk/article-research-shows-majority-women-struggle-self-esteem

48. How negative feedback impacts women and men differently. (2022, November 8). Quartz. https://qz.com/work/2093763/how-negative-feedback-impacts-women-differently

49. Self confidence statistics UK 2021 - 2022. (2023, May 11). Gee Hair. https://geehair.com/blogs/blog/self-confidence-statistics-uk-2021-2022

50. What is the law of attraction? (2007, February 18). Verywell Mind. https://www.verywellmind.com/understanding-and-using-the-law-of-attraction-3144808

51. Affirmations and Neuroplasticity. (n.d.). Psychology Today. https://www.psychologytoday.com/us/blog/anxiety-another-name-pain/202001/affirmations-and-neuroplasticity

52. Nuclear fusion. (2021, April 2). SpringerLink. https://link.springer.com/referenceworkentry/10.1007/978-1-4614-6431-0_31-3

53. What is entanglement and why is it important? (n.d.). Caltech Science Exchange. https://scienceexchange.caltech.edu/topics/quantum-science-explained/entanglement

54. Evidence of common ancestry and diversity | manoa.hawaii.edu/ExploringOurFluidEarth. (n.d.). https://manoa.hawaii.edu/exploringourfluidearth/biological/invertebrates/evidence-common-ancestry-and-diversity

55. The Big Bang. (2023, March 7). Exploratorium. https://www.exploratorium.edu/explore/origins/big-bang

56. Forest bathing. (2020, March 29). Chronicle Online. https://www.chronicleonline.com/news/real_estate/forest-bathing/article_ae3daec2-708c-11ea-9ee5-67eacea8fe78.html#

57. Davis, S. (2021, May 11). The psychology behind why we love completing to-dos| blog. Workast | The Best Project Management Tool for Slack Teams - Try it Today!. https://www.workast.com/blog/the-secret-psychology-on-why-we-love-completing-to-do-lists/

58. The power of small wins. (2011, May 1). Harvard Business Review. https://hbr.org/2011/05/the-power-of-small-wins

59. Life crafting as a way to find purpose and meaning in life. (n.d.). PubMed Central (PMC). https://www.ncbi.nlm.nih.gov/pmc/articles/PMC6923189/

60. Building your resilience. (2012, January 1). https://www.apa.org. https://www.apa.org/topics/resilience/building-your-resilience

61. United Nations. (n.d.). Malala Yousafzai. https://www.un.org/en/messengers-peace/malala-yousafzai

62. Contributions of attachment theory and research: A framework for future research, translation, and policy. (n.d.) https://www.ncbi.nlm.nih.gov/pmc/articles/PMC4085672/

63. How to train our brain: Learn, unlearn, relearn. (2022, December 15). Arhitectura & Design - Spatii Educationale | Regandim spatiile educationale pentru secolul XXI. https://pavonistudio.com/how-to-train-our-brain-learn-unlearn-relearn/

64. Brown, B. (n.d.). The power of vulnerability. TED: Ideas Worth Spreading. https://www.ted.com/talks/brene_brown_the_power_of_vulnerability?language=en

www.ingramcontent.com/pod-product-compliance
Lightning Source LLC
LaVergne TN
LVHW010720061126
851857LV00014B/1272
9798230296553